ESSAYS AND STUDIES
1973

ESSAYS AND STUDIES
1973

BEING VOLUME TWENTY-SIX OF THE NEW SERIES
OF ESSAYS AND STUDIES COLLECTED FOR
THE ENGLISH ASSOCIATION

BY JOHN LAWLOR

JOHN MURRAY

FIFTY ALBEMARLE STREET LONDON

Printed in Great Britain by
Cox & Wyman Ltd, London, Fakenham and Reading

0 7195 2864 X

Contents

Honour in Chaucer

D. S. BREWER

THE vagaries of the notion of honour are complex in English, different from Continental notions, and of great human importance and literary interest. Chaucer mentions honour frequently and creates a characteristically rich and subtle concept, which it is essential to understand for appreciation especially of *Troilus and Criseyde*, but also of several other poems, and of Chaucer's own literary personality.[1]

The duality of honour strikes any reader of Chaucer, or of earlier English literature, rather more strongly than readers of

[1] The study of the treatment of honour in English literature was introduced into English criticism by Professor E. M. Wilson in this same series: 'Family Honour in the Plays of Shakespeare's Predecessors and Contemporaries', *Essays and Studies 1953*, pp. 19–40. There is more extensive study of honour in Spanish literature (cf. M. R. L. De Malkiel, *La Idea de la Fama en la Edad Media Castellana*, Pánuco, Mexico, 1952 – a reference I owe to Professor Wilson). But Wilson shows that honour in Spanish differs in important ways from that in English sixteenth-century drama. C. L. Barber makes a valuable survey, *The Idea of Honour in the English Drama 1591–1700*, Göteborg, 1957. G. F. Jones comments on some aspects of honour from St. Augustine onwards as a background to his discussion of Lovelace in 'Lov'd I Not Honour More: the Durability of a Literary Motif', *Comparative Literature* XI (1959), 131–43. See also C. B. Watson, *Shakespeare and the Renaissance Concept of Honor*, Princeton, 1960, and the suggestive essay on honour in Spanish literature by Professor J. Pitt-Rivers in *Honour and Shame. The Values of Mediterranean Society*, ed. J. G. Peristiany, 1966, pp. 19–78. The Introduction, pp. xxix–xlv to Gavin Douglas, *Shorter Poems*, ed. P. J. Bawcutt, Scottish Text Society, Edinburgh, 1967, has valuable comments on the background to Douglas's *Palice of Honour*. D. S. Brewer studies honour in Malory in the Introduction, pp. 25–35, to Sir Thomas Malory, *The Morte Darthur, Parts Seven and Eight*, 1968. W. Héraucourt, *Die Wertwelt Chaucers*, Heidelberg, 1939, offers some brief interesting comments. Earlier drafts of the present essay were delivered as lectures in Oxford in 1971 and Leeds in 1972, and some main points in abbreviated form are included in D. S. Brewer *Chaucer* 3rd (supplemented) edition, 1973.

Continental literature.[1] In English, and notably in Chaucer, honour is Janus-faced. On the one side honour looks towards goodness, virtue, an inner personal quality; on the other side looks towards social or external reputation, to marks of dignity, like giving generous feasts, or making honorific gestures like kneeling. Honour in terms of virtue perhaps reaches its highest expression when the Virgin herself is described as *honour*, and root of goodness after Christ (*CT.* VII, 463–5).[2] She is also described as the *honour of mankind* (*CT.* VII, 619). Such expressions are not reducible to any clear scheme in their own terms, though they are based on the association of female honour with chastity. Each aspect of the expression, the Virgin, and honour, is conceived of as the highest value, and each reflects glory on the other. To be honourable or worshipped is always to be approved. More clearly in a schematic way, Chaucer's translation of the *De Consolatione Philosophiae* of Boethius (henceforth referred to as *Boece*) makes *propre honour* synonomous with intrinsic personal virtue (*Boece* IV, p. 3, 27).

At the other extreme, that of social reputation, *Boece* makes equally clear in Book III, proses 2 and 4, which particularly discuss honour, that *to be holden honourable or reverent ne cometh nat to folk of hir propre strengthe of nature, but oonly of the false opynyoun of folk* (III, p. 4, 73), which Criseyde would have done well to remember. Honour may consist only of the externals, of *dignytees*, which are good in themselves, it is assumed (and certainly many people are said by Lady Philosophy to believe) but which are trivial, and are *yyven ofte to wikkide men* (IV, p. 4, 10). Honour therefore, of this kind, is an earthly good, and like all such goods is for Boethius a real good, but also really bad, in that such earthly goods are only a sort of parody of the divine goodness, and may deflect us from achieving that; they are appearance rather than reality. This

---

[1] *OED* is useful, and reveals the range of concepts, but not surprisingly may often be questioned in its allocation of significances of this extraordinarily slippery word. The notion of G. F. Jones *art. cit.* that a single vocable expresses two dissimilar concepts avoids rather than solves the problem.

[2] All citations (but not their punctuation) are from Chaucer's *Works*, ed. F. N. Robinson, 2nd ed. 1957. The abbreviation *CT* is used for *The Canterbury Tales*, with its fragments and lines numbered according to Robinson's edition.

double stage of goodness is an essential element of the *Boece*, as I believe it is of the *Troilus*. It inheres in the vocabulary and confuses discussion because such a word as *dignyte* (e.g. III, p. 4, 102) may mean either '*dignyte* as normally and erroneously conceived in the world of appearances' or 'true *dignyte*', which may often appear to the worldly eye as no *dignyte* at all. But in the case of honour the confusing but not necessarily confused or mistaken duality of appearance and reality is built deep into Chaucer's and our culture, and as a general concept cannot be divided. External reputation would be nothing if it did not impute and by intention confirm internal virtue, however often mistakenly. Internal virtue would not have the power and implications essential to it if it did not in some ways appear, and be honoured for what it was when it did appear. Yet external honour may be even a danger to internal worth, as *Boece* makes clear, and as becomes explicit in religious terms when Melibeus is told by his admirable wife Prudence that he has so much enjoyed, among other delights, *honours of this world*, that he has forgotten Jesus Christ his creator (*CT* VII, 1411).

Nevertheless the continuum of meaning between intrinsic worth and external reputation, dignity and reward, is not hard to understand. Appearance *ought* to coincide with reality, and though we know that often or usually it does not, we ought to try to make it do so. Prudence tells Melibeus that

> he sholde not be called a gentil man that, after God and good conscience, alle thynges left, ne dooth his diligence and bisynesse to kepen his good name.

And she quotes Solomon for support on the value of a good name as being above great riches. (1635–41.) 'Good name' is not so loaded a term as 'honour', but numerous passages and collocations show that it is a near synonym. Prudence goes on to quote, quite correctly, a sermon by St. Augustine which says, with supporting quotations from 2nd Corinthians VIII, 21, and 2nd Titus II, 7, that we have a duty to preserve both good conscience and good name, Latin *fama*. (*Sermo* CCCLV, PL 39, *c*. 1568). St.

Thomas Aquinas expresses the duality in a more unified form, though this does not appear explicitly in Chaucer.[1] Honour is by no means necessarily un-Christian in its full formulation. As it faces internally, it supports virtue; as it faces externally, it respects virtue in others and reports, for the respect of others, the inner virtue of the bearer.

Honour, therefore, is not so much a virtue as an activity, perhaps like courage, which should support virtue, but does not always do so. The verbs *honour, worship* are always used in a good sense in Chaucer and may be both religious and secular.

Self-forgetful yet deeply satisfying as this human quality of paying honour is in itself, it has a further important component easily overlooked today; that of belonging to a group, to some extent self-selected, of which the members have something fundamental in common. To pay honour to someone is to associate oneself with him or her, and of course with other worshippers too, so that in some senses, to pay honour is also to receive it, provided your honouring is accepted. If you do not pay honour, or if it is not accepted, you are outside the honour-group.

Honour also contributes to the sense of personal identity which is a product of both internal and social forces. A man must be able to answer for himself and be recognizable as what he is, in order to be approved. If one loses one's name, one loses honour, one's place in the honour-group and thus in society. One's function becomes uncertain. In the end, honour comes close to identity, particularly when that is conceived in terms of social relationships.

It is important to notice that to *be* honourable is to love *trouthe*, not to love *honour*, and again honour if analysed is not exactly a virtue but a maintenance of virtue. The possible divergence between honour and virtue becomes of great importance in certain contexts. Here we may note, what has been extremely important for English culture far beyond the bounds of literature, that the king in England is not presented as the fount of honour, as Wilson points out he is in Spanish literature, any more than he is above the law, as according to Pitt-Rivers he also is in Spanish

[1] *A Lexicon of St. T. Aquinas*, ed. R. J. Deferrari, I. Barry, I. McGuiness, Catholic University of America Press, 1948, p. 489.

literature. Therefore, though he should be a type of honour he is not in any way above the honour-system, as he is in Spanish. Wilson notes that in English Renaissance drama, too, honour does not derive from the king but is a perquisite of noblemen. In Chaucer, it seems, honour derives from the public recognition of virtue, as in Arcite's case when under the name of Philostrate he achieves honour in the court of Theseus. Honour therefore arises as a tacit understanding in the 'honour-group', *gentils of honour* (III, 1209), according to the expression in *The Wife of Bath's Tale*. But the honour-group may exclude the regular clergy on the one hand, and, to judge from the absence of reference to honour and the positive evidence of their activities, it excludes on the other hand millers, carpenters, manciples, university men and *swich rascaille*.

The edges of the group are blurred as so often in English society, for perhaps the honour-group includes the Pardoner, since he, with his superficial social morality, in his bogus sermon, condemns drunkenness and gambling not as vices, but as dishonour, as shame (*CT.* VI, 580, 595), and commends the Ten Commandments as *honourable* (*CT.* VI, 640) which the Parson does not. However, the Parson himself condemns lechery as depriving both man and woman of good fame and *al hire honour* which enables the devil to win *the mooste partie of this world* (*CT.* X, 847–50). Although the Parson attributes to *the prophete* this fairly comprehensive denial of true honour, the source has not been traced and the sentiment could be Chaucer's own. It may still be dramatically suited to the Parson. The same sentiment about lechery is attributed to Cenobia in *The Monk's Tale* (VII, 2293), even in marriage. Whether it represents the secularization of religious values or the sanctification of a secular concept of honour I leave it to others to decide. What we may well think is that, as with the Prioress, this religious notion of lechery as dishonour is only partially applicable to the general honour-system, and is probably more religious and female than male.

Honour also can be inherited from ancestors (*CT.* VII, 2197–8, 2643) and this concept is never attacked as the closely connected notion of inheriting *gentillesse* is attacked in *The Wife of Bath's*

Tale. Honour is a more social concept than *gentillesse* and it holds the group together not only at the present moment but also in time, from ancestor to descendant. Inheritance of honour also firmly establishes the existence of the sub-group of the family within the larger honour-group.

Within the large honour-group of the *gentils* are two very important major sub-groups, for whom the practice of honour, so far discussed in general terms, is very different. They are, naturally, men and women, or rather, knights and ladies. We become vividly aware of the biological base of what has so far been discussed in social and moral terms. The honour of knights rests on the dominant biological characteristic of most young men, their aggressiveness. Honour institutionalizes a vital but unruly and often destructive element in young men, and so to some extent controls and directs it into socially useful channels, that is, the defence of the group against external aggression, or at least into socially if not physically harmless activities like sport, such as jousting. This is how honour not only cements the group together but offers social approval for the biological masculine role, and contributes to the knight's sense of identity and social function. A knight acquires *honour and worship* essentially by fighting bravely, by the exercise of arms, which is his predominant duty. In Arveragus's case in *The Franklin's Tale* it takes him away from the wife to whom he is utterly devoted for two years and there is no suggestion within the poem that he ought to do otherwise. His absence is the measure of his devotion. 'I could not love thee, dear, so much, Lov'd I not honour more.' Arcite's acquisition of honour is more vague and more civilian (his career as a courtier is curiously parallel to Chaucer's own), but though he wins honour partly by 'his good tongue' (eloquence being important in Chaucer's knightly ideal), he also wins honour by 'deeds'. (*CT.* I, 1438). Honour for a man is primarily based on military prowess, which is often the meaning of *worthynesse* (*LGW* 1648; cf. *CT.* I, 3060). There is nothing surprising in all this. What is notable about Chaucer is that he, in that chivalric fourteenth-century court, shows practically no interest in military prowess. Nevertheless he accepts it unequivocally as a high moral ideal and this most ironic and satirical poet never mocks bravery. To be called a coward is intolerable in Chaucer, though oddly enough most of the occurrences of the word occur in marital or sexual contexts, except for the Parson, who is unexceptionably martial – it is a *coward champioun recreant that seith 'creant' withoute nede* (*CT.* x, 695–700). According to Pandarus, too, it is no honour for a man to weep (*Troilus*, v, 408), though Pandarus, that man of action not of feeling, is usually impatient of weeping anyway (i, 697–702).

Except by Pandarus, who can hardly be called a man of honour (amongst other reasons, he never does any fighting), it seems generally agreed that in one situation timidity on the part of a knight is a virtue—that is, when he falls in love. In *The Book of the Duchess* the Knight's boldness when he meets his lady is turned to *shame* (617, 1213) and so is Troilus's. *Shame* comes to mean modesty, Shakespeare's 'maiden shame' more usually attributed to ladies. In Chaucer we have here an extension of that ancient European concept, which has strong Christian connotations, of the knight who is a lion in the field, and a lamb in hall among ladies. (It is not absolutely gone. An obituary, published in *The Times* of August 1972, of a winner of the Victoria Cross in the war of 1939–45 records an identical pattern.) Chaucer's young men are in sexual matters paradoxically the less aggressive the more honourable they are, and the extreme instance is Arveragus who rejects honour for *trouthe*. One must not make this too moralistic. Sex has not much to do with honour for young knights. The rapist knight in *The Wife of Bath's Tale* is never described as dishonourable, though he has committed a despicable crime. What is dishonourable is to be a traitor (e.g. *CT.* i, 1129–32) but if no promise has been made, no treachery is involved. It cannot be said that it is *generally* accepted in Chaucer's poetry, any more than in the Western tradition as a whole, that to debauch and destroy a woman is regarded as dishonourable. Honour here diverges from virtue and justice and of course from the teachings of Christianity, and perhaps the most that can be said is that Chaucer more nearly associates honour with virtue in this respect than do Continental writers.

B

Nevertheless love in Chaucer is a very different matter from sex, especially for women, as will be shown, but also for men. A knight may be shy with ladies, and yet passionately in love, like the Black Knight in *The Book of the Duchess*, and Troilus. Troilus seems to be sexually innocent. A knight will grow in honour simply by being in love, as the poet suggests (I, 251) that Troilus tells himself hopefully at the beginning of his love (I, 374–6); and as seems to be born out when successful though secret love so increases his honour that it rings to the very gate of heaven (III, 1723) (though a knight has to be in an honourable state to start with for his honour to increase by love).

But it is striking that whereas Criseyde shows intense concern for what people will say, and for social and indeed moral obligations (in this respect typical of all Chaucer's ladies, though she is a significantly extreme example), Troilus is quite ready for Criseyde's sake to desert the Trojan cause, to which he is so necessary, without a moment's thought. Arcite also in *The Knight's Tale* says he will gladly forgo his honour if only he can please Emily (*CT*. I, 711). There is apparently no great clash between love and honour in Chaucer as there is in Spanish and perhaps other Continental literature, because love, not honour, is taken by young men as the supreme value. Indeed, just as Troilus's honour is increased with his successful love, Troilus, when he hears that Criseyde must go to the Greeks, says that he has fallen out of honour into misery (IV, 271). Troilus equates successful love with his good fortune and both with honour; his ill-fortune in love is to him loss of honour. This view of honour as secondary to love, yet attached to it, sets Chaucer apart from many European writers who have used the concept of honour, and no doubt sets him apart also from the normal social concepts of his own time outside literature. For Troilus the association of love with honour may perhaps be regarded as a sort of serious parody of marriage. Troilus in his absolute fidelity to Criseyde, as also in his invocation of Hymen (III, 1258) and his address to Criseyde as *fresshe wommanliche wif* (III, 1296), imaginatively, but of course erroneously, constantly identifies himself with the married state, as Criseyde rarely does. If Troilus had truly married Criseyde he would have saved himself a lot of trouble in one respect: though he might have found more of a different kind. But the poignancy of the story is precisely that it is *not* about marriage: it is about a love which is largely unsupported by social institutions. The evasion of social institutions of a legitimate kind of course involves the employment of a well-known social institution that is illegitimate, the bawd or pimp, a function to which Pandarus has given his name in English. Chaucer makes Pandarus confess or hint three times how shameful a role this is (II, 355–7; III, 249; V, 1734).

Though Troilus may behave morally as if married he naturally cannot take part in the full honour-structure of the married man. In this the wife shares honour with her husband, and married couples may be said to constitute honour-groups partially within such other honour-groups as the family, and knights, or ladies (*CT.* III, 961–4). A *good* wife confers honour on her husband (*CT.* IV, 133) so that with this qualification marriage itself confers honour on a man. It is specifically the faithfulness of a wife which is an honour to the husband (*CT.* IV, 2171; cf. V, 1358 ff.), but a well-dressed wife is also an honour to her husband (*CT.* VII, 13; *LGW*, 2473), though this of course needs money (*CT.* VII, 408).

The emphasis being on faithfulness, dishonour comes to both husband and wife if *she* commits adultery. An unfaithful wife is described by Hypermnestra as a traytour *lyvynge in my shame* (*LGW*, 2702). This is, or rather was until very recently, so completely accepted in all advanced Western and Eastern cultures, perhaps universally, that it hardly needs illustrating. However a number of modern criticisms of *The Franklin's Tale* underestimate this deep and powerful notion. When Dorigen makes her 'complaint' in her dilemma between death and dishonour, giving a long list of those wives who have chosen death rather than commit even forced adultery, the deliberate artificiality of the passage, which allows us to contemplate the situation with detachment, and even a touch of humour, rather than with inappropriately tragic expectations, is surely not calculated, as some critics think[1], to satirize or raise a trivial snigger. Chaucer in his serious poetry, however, is not much interested in adultery, notwithstanding the astonishing prevalence of the modern notion that medieval love is always adulterous. Troilus and Criseyde are not in a position to commit adultery, and Chaucer mainly writes about adultery as a joke amongst those who have little or no honour, as part of the effect of some of his comic poems, including the Wife of Bath's *Prologue*, though not her *Tale*. Part also of the comedy of the Wife of Bath's reversal of values is that her cowed fifth husband allows her to keep the marital honour (III, 821) and that in her tale the wife is allowed to choose what course of action will be most honour to both her and her husband (III, 1232-3). Once given this choice the wife in the tale chooses to be both fair and good, that is, faithful, and to *obey* her husband in everything he wants. Honour is interchanged. In the comic poems proper January of course loses honour when cuckolded, but that is his own fault and serves him right for being a lecherous as well as a silly old man. May is also dishonoured, but she is hardly within the honour-group, being *of smal degree* (IV, 1625), not quite a lady. The merchant in *The Shipman's Tale* is only doubtfully a man of honour, since he is not in any way a fighting man, nor associated with men of honour, and his cuckolding is part of other social and moral systems, like the goings-on in *The Miller's* and *The Reeve's Tale*. Adultery within the honour-group therefore hardly arises in Chaucer.

The family as an honour-group may be briefly mentioned here as arising out of marriage. The extended family share their honour, of course, and a man may easily lose honour by the conduct of his unmarried female relatives, even when this is not by their own choice. The outstanding instance is *The Physician's Tale*, where the father kills his daughter to preserve her virginity against tyrannical oppression, thereby preserving her, and consequently his, honour. 'I could not love thee, dear, so much ...' That this story derives from Roman antiquity reminds us again that these concepts are ancient and widespread. Yet a certain mechanical

[1] Fortunately, not including J. Lawlor, *Chaucer*, 1968, who discusses the poem at length.

quality in Chaucer's telling of this story suggests that his imagination was not fully engaged in so simple and traditional a representation of the concept, however completely he may have accepted it.

More interestingly, Pandarus feels dishonoured by Criseyde's behaviour. He perhaps ought to have felt dishonoured by her lechery with Troilus, and perhaps he would have done had it been socially known. What actually troubles him is not her unchastity but her falseness, that other aspect of honour (*Troilus* v, 1727).

We come at last to the honour of ladies, which is much the most interesting in Chaucer. He is notably more orientated towards feminine interests (and indeed superiority) than any other author until Richardson. Honour for ladies resides primarily in their chastity, the biologically determined defensive or recessive virtue that characterizes, or used to characterize, women, to complement the biologically natural aggressive virtue of men. One may here briefly mention what often seems to modern notions unjust, that men may commit adultery, or be sexually promiscuous, without losing honour, while women may not. The reason lies simply with the traditionally accepted truth that men and women are different, and that therefore their honour and identity and virtue have a different base. This also explains the apparent paradox that honourable men may try to seduce honourable women, yet despise them when they succeed. In the process women—not men—lose honour, and so drop out of the honour-group, though they may retain or even increase their attractiveness. Conversely, a woman was not dishonoured by being a coward. The classic comic treatment of the difference in that respect is the 'duel' between Viola and Sir Andrew Aguecheek in *Twelfth Night*. Both are arrant cowards, but Viola only gains in femininity and lovableness with our recognition of her charming cowardice, while we despise, however genially, Sir Andrew. (That Shakespeare also accepted the ideals of other traditional distinctions in honour, including chastity for women, is amply clear, for example in Posthumus Leonatus's praise of Imogen for often rejecting his advances even when they were married.) The church has always partially accepted and partially rejected these very ancient traditional notions.

The reason why the Virgin *is* honour is that she is the supreme exemplar of feminine chastity. For more ordinary ladies their honour is chiefly interesting for its relation to their love of a man. The constant note for Chaucer's heroines from Blanche the Duchess onwards is that they love entirely, always 'saving their honour'. Of Blanche, the Black Knight tells us that she gave him her *mercy*, when she understood his woe and when she understood

> That I ne wilned thyng but god
> And worship, and to kepe hir name
> Over alle thyng, and drede hir shame. (1262–4)

It is Blanche's virtue that no one might do her shame because she loved so well her own name (1017–18), that is, her honour, her very identity, founded upon her chastity (cf. *LGW* 300G, 1812, 2586). The close relationship between being truly known to others and being self-sufficient in one's own integrity is well illustrated here. Chastity, after all, may well concern more than one person, yet is an individualizing concept. The honour-system builds sexuality much more significantly into the role of the integrated female personality than into the male, with good biological reason, it may be thought, though all this is strange to modern literary culture.

Sex and love are differentiated for ladies as for knights, but in a different way. Men's sexuality is accepted; it may become love, with its self-sacrifice, ultimately even sacrificing sexuality and life itself, as in the case of Troilus. But there is never any suggestion that Troilus's or any other young knight's love is not sexual and aiming at sexual possession. For ladies, on the contrary, sexuality at most comes after love, if it comes at all. It comes even for Criseyde *after* love, though perhaps somewhat precipitately. The Wife of Bath is not a lady, and, for her, sex is what she chiefly means by love; which is why she is something of a comic man-eating monster, and why the joke of her tale is partly on her.

In Chaucer, as often traditionally, sexuality is always shameful for women, even in marriage, and though wives are holy things they have to put up with it, as he says in *The Man of Law's Tale* (*CT.* II, 708–14). Following the same line of thought, January, a good conservative, judges that he must offend May on their marriage night with his *corage . . . sharp and keene* (*CT.* IV, 1756–9).

Ladies naturally do not exactly acquire honour any more than they acquire virginity (whereas a knight has to earn his), but they may increase in honour by going up the social scale as Griselda does, and by marrying and being faithful to their husbands. They can lose honour no doubt through poverty or old age or envy, like a man, but the interesting way to lose it is by being known to have a lover, if unmarried, or if married by committing adultery, which is represented as treachery, the height of medieval vice which absorbs other delinquencies into it. 'Falseness' is both sin and shame.

Death should be preferable to dishonour for both knight and lady but as it was a normal occupational hazard for knights it seems more significant, perhaps because usually more volitional, for ladies, as *The Physician's Tale* shows in the death of Virginia, and as Dorigen represents in her long list of examples of the death of virtuous wronged ladies. Troilus says he himself would rather die than cause *disclaundre* to Criseyde's name, though Criseyde herself does not express such heroic sentiment.

The consideration of Criseyde's honour weighs more heavily with both Troilus and Criseyde than anything else, even their love, as Book IV frequently shows. Ladies have a very high degree of responsibility for their own honour, even when married, and for a widow in Criseyde's position, and with her temperament, it may well be—ironically—her chief concern. Criseyde looks after her own honour very assiduously (e.g. II, 468; III, 944). She is always talking about it, and it is far more crucial to the story and the poem than is often realized. A word-count illustrates this in a crude but effective fashion. There are forty-seven occurrences of the word *honour* in *Troilus and Criseyde*. No less than twenty-six occur in connection with Criseyde, and seven of these are references by herself to her own honour. By contrast only nine occurrences of the word refer to Troilus, and not one of these is

a reference made by himself. The remaining twelve occurrences
are a miscellaneous scatter, four of them in reference to the gods.
Of eight references by a person to 'my honour' seven are those
by Criseyde as already mentioned, and the eighth by whom but
Pandarus. In whichever way one analyses the totality of references in the poem to honour, Criseyde dominates them. It is after
all in some respects a poem about her honour, or rather, her
dishonour.

Since honour must be shared, and a lady's honour is sexual,
she shares her honour with the man with whom she has sexual
intercourse. In the case of marriage this is socially recognized and
the source of increased honour to them both. If the lady is not
married the sharing is secret and therefore more complex. She is
in her lover's power, since if he boasts of his conquest she loses
her honour, as Criseyde tells Troilus (III, 165, cf. v, 1077). Criseyde
anxiously and absurdly talks of her own *honeste* which elsewhere
means chastity (as in *LGW* 1673), when the context shows that
she really has in mind, as usual, what people will think of her.
How foully my *honeste* will be spotted, she says, if I go away with
you. I should never regain my *name*—and *name* clearly here
means honour and the reputation for chastity (as in *LGW* 301G,
1812, 2587). Criseyde argues that if she eloped with Troilus, as
his mistress—and no alternative status is ever envisaged by either—
she would lose her honour, that is, her place in society, her very
identity. She is a very conventional young woman, and she is
quite right. Would they pass their lives in some Black Sea holiday
resort? Benjamin Constant's *Adolphe* and Tolstoy's *Anna Karenina*
are both parables, set in societies whose values differed astonish-
ingly little from those of fourteenth-century England in this
respect, of what happens to lovers who are unsupported by the
institutions of society and where the man's—like Othello's—
occupation's gone. Criseyde has no need to doubt Troilus's
entire devotion to her, but that is not the only point for her.
Because she has always found him true she says that she will
always behave

That ay honour to me-ward shal rebounde (IV, 1666).

She seems self-regarding, but in a sense she has to be. She needs social support and a social contract. Pandarus has betrayed her, and even Troilus's devotion is based on a relationship which if known would dishonour her though not him. It is true that later she regrets not eloping with Troilus (v, 739–40) and remarks that one should not pay attention to what people say, but she is already by this time on the downward path, and anyway under no risk of having to do anything. When she is told she must leave Troy the poor girl is in a cleft stick and honour is the source of the profound irony of her fate as a literary figure. She who is more interested in her own honour than any other character in Chaucer, or in English literature except Richardson's heroines, is represented in the poem as *the* person in history who has lost her honour. She has put external social worldly reputation before the internal value of *trouthe* to Troilus and has ironically lost the external reputation just because she preferred it. To prefer appearance to reality is to lose both. But the reason that she is in a cleft stick is more complex still, because she has become confused about the nature of honour. She has applied, in a sense, the wrong sort of honour to herself. She has constantly retained the view that her honour consists in her chastity, as an unmarried woman. But her relationship with Troilus has changed her status in practice if not overtly and socially. She is judged in the poem *as if she were married*, though she is never represented during the poem as being quite as devoted to Troilus as he to her. Still, she has twice made vows of unending fidelity to Troilus (III, 1492 ff.; IV, 1534 ff.), and she is judged according to her own expressed intention. A married woman's honour is judged by her loyalty to her husband, and Criseyde, who is not married, is yet judged not for her lack of chastity, but for her falseness, her lack of *trouthe*.

> She seyde, 'Allas, for now is clene ago
> My name of trouthe in love for everemo. (v, 1054–5)

One might say that if she goes away with Troilus she is dishonoured in the eyes of society for her unchastity; and if she abandons Troilus she is dishonoured in the eyes of the poet and his readers for her lack of *trouthe*. The poem curiously and in a way inconsistently bridges two worlds here, Criseyde's public world, and her private one. Within the public world of the poem Criseyde's loss of honour could only occur in relation to her seduction by Diomede, as a loss of chastity which—her dead husband apart—she had already secretly lost to Troilus. But poet and readers may think they perceive the inner value, the personal loyalty, *trouthe*, based on, but transcending, physical relationship, which Criseyde has broken.

As we hear in *The Franklin's Tale*

Trouthe is the hyeste thyng that man may kepe, (v, 1479)

or woman either, we must add. *The Franklin's Tale* is explicitly about *trouthe*'s superiority to honour. The poem is of course artificial in the same way that a folk-tale or a parable is artificial: it is not an illusionist transcript of ordinary life but a narrated series of events and characters put together to make a specific point about life, often the more penetrating because of the primary limitations in literary convention. Once these have been accepted however, as any ordinarily experienced reader, who does not have to make a living by publishing critical essays, normally does accept them, the poem has plenty of witty observation of ordinary life, and a strong sense of reality.

At the beginning Arveragus in his happy marriage keeps the appearance of sovereignty in marriage because of his honour as a knight—*for shame of his degree* (v, 752) as we are told by the poet (and here as so often in *The Canterbury Tales* we are justified in disregarding in such details the 'dramatic narrator', in this case the Franklin, whose function has for the moment ceased). Arveragus like a proper knight values his honour and in order to acquire more (v, 811–2) goes abroad. As with the false knight in *The Squire's Tale*, but without reference to falseness,

resoun wolde eek that he moste go
For his honour, as ofte it happeth so. (v, 591–2)

Dorigen then, pestered by the squire Aurelius, to soften her absolute refusal of love with a sophisticated joke which she rightly later regrets, says she will give herself to Aurelius if he removes the rocks on the coast which threaten her beloved husband's safe return. Once this is apparently done she is trapped, having promised dishonour for honourable reasons; promised treachery out of faith. There are many rich implications here which must be left aside. In the matter of honour, when Arveragus returns safely and the squire's bargain is apparently fulfilled, the first point to note is that Dorigen at last gives to her husband the reality, not just the appearance, of sovereignty when she asks him what to do about Aurelius. Honour rightly undertakes responsibility and receives sovereignty in marriage. When Arveragus decides, with grief, that Dorigen ought to keep her promise, her *trouthe* to Aurelius, he is thus ironically and paradoxically forced to resign that honour, so important to him, which he now truly possesses, and which resides in his wife's faithfulness to him, just now so touchingly demonstrated, in order that she, on behalf of both of them, shall keep her paradoxical *trouthe*, her promise to commit adultery with Aurelius. She has to accept her own dishonour because it would be dishonourable not to: it is a shame to a woman to trick a man, it is said (admittedly by Pandarus, *Troilus* III, 777). *Trouthe* is loyalty, and in the cluster of notions that compose the sentiment of honour, the keeping of *trouthe* must be isolated as so much the superior inner moral value as to be, as on this occasion, positively hostile to social relationship and reputation. It was this complexity that poor Criseyde failed to observe. But the exquisite delicacy of the sacrifice cannot be appreciated if we forget or deny the other elements of honour, bravery and chastity, the shame of cuckoldry and of pandarism (for does not Arveragus *send* his wife to Aurelius?), the shame of sex for women, the pain of loss of social reputation. Indeed Arveragus shows no exaggerated heroism, for he hopes that the whole business can be kept as quiet as possible, though the true inner situation is what appals him, not the appearance only (v, 1481–6). The interest lies in the way that the ironic paradox of dishonour rooted in honour is poetically incarnate in a living culture. Honour as social virtue,

and honour as chastity or possession, are subordinated to honour
as obedience to a high moral ideal, perforce an inner, indeed, a
spiritual value. The story of course is given a happy ending. In
Chaucer's fundamentally optimistic Christian culture goodness
brings forth goodness. The story shows how sacrifice creates
happiness. Sexual jealousy and possessiveness, personal domina-
tion, narrow legalism, are all rejected in favour of openness,
truth, loyalty, trust, toleration and love.

Of course we must accept the primary conventions. In real life,
we might ask that the long-term promise given by Dorigen to
her husband when she married him take precedence over the
short-term and obviously joking promise made to Aurelius. But
that would be to judge the poem by the totally inappropriate
premises of the realistic novel, which are never even accidentally
invoked by Chaucer, for all his realism.

This spiritualization of honour was not a late development in
Chaucer. It was inherent in the complex religious and secular
tradition of many centuries, though Chaucer creates his own
individual and characteristic forms. He had earlier, in *The House
of Fame*, taken to himself as poet the internalized stability and
confidence that his greatest heroine so clearly lacks, showing in
his own self something of that carelessness of honour as reputation
that his heroes possess, or perhaps indicating that he himself, for
all his interest, is really outside the honour-system, being no
knight, no fighting-man. If so, it may be one reason for his
modernity, for the honour-system in England, never so strong as
on the Continent, has surely now collapsed. Yet modernity cannot
be too easily claimed, for the Church had in certain respects for
many centuries denied the value of honour. Lydgate the monk has
a dreary little poem (founded, as Skeat noted, on an earlier Latin
line) which says that four things make a man a fool; age, women,
wine—and honour (*Chaucerian and Other Pieces*, 1897, pp. l–li,
297). Yet even Lydgate may well be more modern than he looks.

In that strange poem *The House of Fame*, the poet (and I call him
the poet, not that man of straw, the so-called Narrator of many
modern critics) is asked, Don't you care what people think of you?
He replies

Sufficeth me, as I were ded,
That no wight have my name in honde. (1876–7)

It rings very true; and when we consider that his name is more
than ever in hand, nearly six centuries after his death, it constitutes
the most delightful of Chaucerian paradoxes.

II

The Pursuit of Relevance

KENNETH MUIR

THE demand for relevance in literature, and especially in drama, takes a variety of forms. It is apparent in the way in which under-graduates pick modern optional courses, in their plea that Orwell and Miller should replace Yeats and Conrad in the syllabus, in the popularity of 'sociology of literature' courses, in Brecht's rewriting of *Coriolanus* to make it more relevant to the political situation in the present century, in Günter Grass's *The Plebeians Rehearse the Uprising*, in the tendency of theatre directors to present the classics in modern dress, and in their admiration for Jan Kott's theories.

In some ways this desire for relevance is healthy. It springs from a distrust of a literature divorced from life. After all, it is generally accepted that the novel should offer a relevant criticism of life; that *Vanity Fair*, for example, although set in the past, was not irrelevant to the Victorian present, nor to ours; that *Felix Holt*, another historical novel, was as relevant as *Silas Marner*; and that Dickens in all his novels, and especially in the later, greater ones, had a powerful message for his age—he wanted to reform the world by showing us what was wrong with it. On the other hand, the plays of Victorian poets—Tennyson's *Becket*, Browning's *King Victor and King Charles*, Swinburne's plays on Mary, Queen of Scots, Bridges' *Palicio*, even Hardy's *Famous Tragedy of the Queen of Cornwall*—had little to say to their own age, and nothing to say to us. Elizabethan dramatists rarely made this kind of mistake. Not merely did Jonson, we are told, give an allegorical account of the Gunpowder Plot in *Catiline*, and Shakespeare introduce allusions to the same plot in *Macbeth*—to remind the audience that king-killing could happen in 1605 as it had done in Scotland 'in the dark backward and abysm of time'—

but even Lyly's delicate and artificial structures were as topical as the Goon Show. It was not simply that by the deliberate use of anachronism Elizabethan dramatists called attention to parallels between ancient and modern. Historians, no less than dramatists, were all anxiously didactic, satisfying the voracious appetites of their readers for facts about the past, at the same time as they were exhibiting the workings of Providence (as Ralegh did in his great Preface), or pointing out the horrors of civil war and the blessings of the Tudor settlement; or even, as Machiavelli did in his *Discourses on Livy*, using particular events to illustrate general historical or political principles. It can easily be seen that in the English Histories, besides writing exciting and popular entertainment, Shakespeare was using the past to influence the present. It is assumed that *A Midsummer Night's Dream* contains allusions to the bad weather of 1594; it has been plausibly maintained that *King Lear* exhibited the dangers of a divided kingdom at the time when James I was advocating the union of England and Scotland; and it has often been suggested that *Coriolanus* took the form it did because of the Midlands insurrection.

In two of his Roman plays Shakespeare makes his characters allude to the future dramatization of the events in which they are concerned. Cleopatra is terrified lest some squeaking actor should boy her greatness in the posture of a whore; and Cassius, carried away by the solemnity of an historical occasion, exclaims:

> How many ages hence
> Shall this our lofty scene be acted over
> In states unborn and accents yet unknown!

Brecht-minded commentators have assumed that in both cases Shakespeare was deliberately shattering the illusion and reminding his audience that they were listening to a play. This, surely, was the precise opposite of what he was doing. The reaction of his original audience—although it is dangerous to generalize about its members—would be to think: 'Yes, that is exactly what is happening; the murder of Julius Caesar *is* being enacted in accents unknown to the Romans, in what was then a barbarous island, as

Cassius foretold, and therefore the play is true. A boy actor is playing Cleopatra now, even as she speaks these words, although happily he has not got a squeaky voice, and this paradoxically establishes the truth of the character who prophesied it.' Even though the temporary effect may be to remind the audience they are watching a play, the ultimate effect will be to reimpose the theatrical illusion more securely than before. It may be added that all the main characters in *Julius Caesar* seem to be conscious of the fact that future ages will be the audience of their lofty scene: they are acting for posterity. Coriolanus postulates an even loftier audience; the culmination of his many theatrical images is when he thinks of himself as having an audience of gods:

> Behold, the heavens do ope,
> The gods look down, and this unnatural scene
> They laugh at.

It is important to realize, however, that neither the cunning use of anachronism, nor even the use of historical material to express orthodox views on order, were the most important means employed by Shakespeare for the achieving of relevance. If that had been so, directors would have been justified, now that anachronisms are explained in footnotes and Tudor views on politics are as quaint as the honour of Marvell's mistress, in seeking some other way of making the plays relevant to a modern audience.

A play which is merely a careful historical reconstruction, or even a competent dramatization of an historical event, of no special relevance to the thought of the day, is doomed to failure. In this connection it may be worth while to compare three plays about Becket. Tennyson's play, saved from disaster by Irving's acting, is unlikely to find an audience again, though it was revived at Canterbury in living memory. Whereas *In Memoriam*, concerned as it was with the doubts and difficulties of Victorians, spoke directly to their hearts, and King Arthur, in the *Idylls of the King*, could be regarded as the embodiment of popular ideals, *Becket* seems to be completely removed from the interests of a nineteenth-century reader. T. S. Eliot did not make this mistake. *Murder in the Cathedral* was written for performance in Canterbury Cathedral before a nominally religious audience, one that could be relied upon to have a kind of domestic interest in the martyrdom of the local saint. The subject of the play, moreover, involved two themes in which Eliot was deeply interested—the relationship between Church and State and the nature of sainthood. One has only to think of *The Idea of a Christian Society* and *The Cocktail Party* to see how these themes continued to engage his interest. Unfortunately Eliot, who had had little dramatic experience, seems to have lost his nerve. He was afraid that his audience would fail to see the relevance of his play to the world of 1935; so he made the four murderers address the audience in speeches which parodied the clichés of modern oratory. Either Eliot, or his producer, made one of the knights wear plus-fours and practise golf strokes. The audience was told that if they approved of the subordination of the Church to the State, they shared the guilt of Becket's murderers. Whatever one may think of this, the speeches are funny in themselves and they jolt the audience out of its complacent reverence; but they are nevertheless a worse blemish than the feeble farce which mars the sublimity of *Saint Joan*. Anouilh's *Becket*, though inferior to Eliot's play in poetic quality and high seriousness, nevertheless appeals more to a modern secular audience, not by drawing parallels between Becket's day and ours, but by showing that the relationship between Becket and the King can be interpreted in modern psychological terms, and related therefore to the experience of members of the audience. There is sexual rivalry in the play and incidental comments on the treatment of subject-races and of women.

Quite apart, then, from any special interest a play may have when it is first performed, it may well appeal to later ages for different reasons. The scenes in *Venice Preserved* which were designed to satirize Shaftesbury's sexual tastes have been successful on the modern stage; but often, when the topical interest fades, the play becomes a bore. Middleton's *Game of Chess*, phenomenally successful in its day, and brilliantly ingenious as it is, did not

survive for many months; and Addison's *Cato*, that extreme
example of neo-classical flummery, was applauded only for
party reasons. On the other hand, *Julius Caesar* remains viable on
stage and screen because Shakespeare convinces us that this is
how men in such circumstances do behave. Brutus, for example,
who fears that a crown will turn Caesar into a tyrant, being
blissfully unaware that he is one already, appears as a timeless
portrait of a political idealist. In *Coriolanus* we can recognize in
the Tribunes some characteristics of demagogues of all ages, no
less than the ignoring of moral scruples characteristic of 'the right-
hand file'. The scene in *Macbeth* between Malcolm and Macduff
used to be criticized as being tedious and improbable; but a
performance just before the Second World War, after the influx
of refugees from Germany, made the scene startlingly realistic.
The fear of betrayal and the report on the state of the nation no
longer sounded exaggerated:

> Alas, poor country,
> Almost afraid to know itself! It cannot
> Be call'd our mother, but our grave; where nothing,
> But who knows nothing, is once seen to smile;
> Where sighs, and groans, and shrieks, that rent the air,
> Are made, not mark'd; where violent sorrow seems
> A modern ecstasy; the dead man's knell
> Is there scarce ask'd for who; and good men's lives
> Expire before the flowers in their caps,
> Dying or ere they sicken.

Directors, to their credit, have recognized the essential truth
in all these cases, and they have sought to make assurance double
sure, so that the audience too will recognize it. Their favourite
method is by the use of modern dress. If Caesar's guards are
dressed as S.S. men, and the conspirators, as in Roy Fuller's
splendid poem, are 'comrades', then the drachma will drop.
Even the dullest members of the audience will thrill to the play's
relevance and return home in the self-congratulatory glow of
people who have taken part in an anti-Nazi demonstration. In
Coriolanus Brutus and Sicinius may be dressed as Bevin or Bevan,

or Scanlon and Feather; Menenius may figure as Baldwin or Macmillan; and Coriolanus can appear as Montgomery or Mussolini, according to political taste.

In the recent National Theatre production of *The Merchant of Venice*, the modern dress of Shylock immediately reminded the audience of the Nazi persecution of the Jews. This was clearly the director's intention, and Shylock emerged as the baffled hero of the play. It need hardly be said that this interpretation runs counter to the text. Shylock's real role is that of villain, as we can see from his first aside:

> How like a fawning publican he looks!
> I hate him for he is a Christian;
> But more for that in low simplicity
> He lends out money gratis, and brings down
> The rate of usance here with us in Venice.
> He hates our sacred nation; and he rails . . .
> On me, my bargains, and my well-won thrift,
> Which he calls interest.

This hatred may spring partly from Antonio's contemptuous rudeness, but it is fanned by religious and especially economic motives. There is nothing in Shakespeare's character to suggest the generous, cultured Jew portrayed by Laurence Olivier: he is a miser, and he hates music—two indications of what the poet thought of him. Of course, there are moments in the play when we are allowed to pity him; but even the scene where he hears of the sale of the ring given him by his dead wife shows that he is more perturbed by the loss of his ducats than of his daughter. If the sympathies of the audience are enlisted for Shylock—because of our modern feelings of guilt—the fourth act will be tragic and the last act will be imbued with bitterness. One can imagine an admirable play in which a noble and cultured Jew is hounded to death by a pack of Philistines, in which Bassanio pursues Portia's fortune rather than her person, in which Jessica is a treacherous thief with Lorenzo her accomplice, and in which the Duke's court is as obviously corrupt as the one where Volpone is tried—but Shakespeare's script cannot be used to mean anything like this. I have more sympathy with the point of view expressed in a recent pamphlet, wrong-headed as it is, that *The Merchant of Venice* should not be staged so long as people remember Belsen and Dachau. One might reply that so long as people remember the concentration camps, the play is unlikely to do any harm.

In defence of adaptations, it has been urged that Shakespeare himself took other men's plays and rewrote them to suit his own purposes, and that therefore Marowitz and others should have the right to adapt Shakespeare's old-fashioned scripts, and so create a new *Hamlet* and a new *Othello*. Directors, retaining the words of the original, should even more clearly have the right to slant the plays to make them relevant to our own time. It may, perhaps, be doubted whether it makes *A Midsummer Night's Dream* more relevant if Hippolyta, that sensible Amazon, is supposed to be cured of her bestial tastes by experiencing as Titania a passion for a donkey. In any case, most people would agree that Shakespeare improved on the old *Hamlet* play and on *Promos and Cassandra*, and few people share Tolstoy's opinion that *King Leir* was better than the play Shakespeare made of it. On the other hand it is by no means certain that the various adaptations of Shakespeare, from Dryden's *Troilus and Cressida* and Tate's *King Lear* to Shaw's *Cymbeline* and Barton's *Wars of the Roses* are improvements on the originals. Shaw, at least, recommends Shakespeare's *Cymbeline* in preference to his own.

A favourite method of bringing home to an audience the relevance of Shakespeare's plays is to associate them with some contemporary fashion. There was a period at Stratford-upon-Avon when nearly every production was adorned or cumbered with a waggon borrowed from *Mother Courage*. This was the outward and visible sign that the history plays were to be treated as epic theatre, complete with *Verfremdungseffekt*. Then we had a diet of Shakespeare the existentialist, with iron in the soul and nausea in the guts. Next we were assured by Jan Kott that *King Lear* was Shakespeare's *End Game*, and that Shakespeare was a proleptic contributor to the Theatre of the Absurd. Finally, under the influence of Artaud and later of Weiss, we were asked to accept him as an honorary member of the Theatre of Cruelty.

Did he not write *Titus Andronicus*? And is not the extrusion of Gloucester's vile jelly more significant than Lear's address to the poor, naked wretches? Kozintsev wisely thought otherwise.

None of these Shakespeares is totally without foundation. There are absurdities and cruelties in *King Lear* and *Titus Andronicus*; but the attempt to present *Macbeth* or *King Lear* in such limited terms immeasurably impoverishes them. If the key-line of *King Lear* is thought to be—

> As flies to wanton boys are we to the gods:
> They kill us for their sport—

Gloucester's later prayer to the 'ever-gentle gods' will seem ironic. The loyalty of Kent, the loving-kindness of Cordelia, the heroism and endurance of Edgar must all appear less significant than the blunt realism of the man who hangs Cordelia. 'If it be man's work, I'll do't.' Gloucester must be thrust out of the castle-gates to smell his way to Dover, but Cornwall's servants must not be allowed the lines in which Shakespeare showed the human-kindness of the humble and made them comment authoritatively and authorially on the wickedness of Regan and Cornwall, as this would undercut the play's cruelty.

Existentialism is not without attractions and it may be said—it has indeed been said by me—that in the world of Elsinore and in the situation in which Hamlet is placed, he has to create his own morality. But whereas Sartre believes that this is the universal state of man, there being no god and no divine sanctions, Hamlet knows that he has to work out his own salvation in fear and trembling. Only in *King Lear* is there any doubt of the existence and nature of the gods; but even if we accept this view of the play, this would not mean that we had the slightest difficulty in distinguishing good from evil. There may be some ambiguity about Shakespeare's metaphysics, but none about his morality.

There are, then, at least four objections to the attempt to impose a modern and arbitrary relevance on an old play. Such an attempt distorts the meaning; insults the intelligence of the audience; substitutes a partial and temporary interpretation for a more universal one; and, as we shall see, it limits the options. These objections overlap. It is not possible to distort the meaning without insulting the audience and if we impose a partial interpretation we obviously limit the options.

Some examples have been given above of directorial distortions. Those responsible presumably fear that audiences would be bored by a straightforward presentation because they themselves have seen the play many times before. Taking Shakespeare's own excuse for his infidelity—

> Like as to make our appetites more keen,
> With eager compounds we our palates urge—

directors offer audiences not Shakespeare's play, but something new and allegedly more relevant. Not that they imagine, as Dryden and Tate apparently did, that they can improve on Shakespeare, excepting in minor details, but they believe that their versions will appeal to an audience more than the originals would do. If one were to judge by the reactions of certain dramatic critics, saved from boredom at their twentieth production of *The Merchant of Venice*, or of some other play that has often been clapper-clawed by the palms of the vulgar, one might suppose that directors were right in their calculations. A tape-recording of audience reactions would tell a very different story. They came to see Shakespeare and, to their disappointment, were given something else, and something inferior.

It is reported in *The Elizabethan Theatre* (edited David Galloway, 1969) that a questionnaire was issued to members of the audience at the Royal Shakespeare Memorial Theatre, in order to discover facts about their social and educational background. Terence Hawkes, in his analysis of the replies, showed that nearly all the respondents were middle-class, two-thirds of them were under thirty, over sixty per cent were teachers or students, and over seventy per cent were graduates, undergraduates, or hoping to enter a university in due course. The significance of these figures is twofold: most of the audience were young enough not to have seen many productions of the plays and their intellectual level was remarkably high. This means that directors at Stratford and at the National Theatre have no need to temper the icy wind of pure Shakespeare to an audience of semi-literate Philistines. They may be as literate as the director himself and quite unlikely to feel that Shakespeare's plays were remote stories of

> old, unhappy, far-off things,
> And battles long ago,

with small relevance to the twentieth-century mind. Such an educated audience is apt to resent both the distortion involved in the modish productions we have been describing and what is surely the arrogant assumption that they would not notice the relevance of *Coriolanus* or of *Troilus and Cressida* unless it is made so blatantly clear that only a moron could miss it. They feel as Queen Victoria's correspondents must have done when they received her epistolary underlinings.

If Coriolanus is depicted as a fascist dictator and the Tribunes as Labour politicians, the audience is thereby prevented from seeing the play steadily and seeing it whole. Between 1609 and 1970 the political changes were so enormous that we can no longer look at the play with Jacobean eyes. In 1609 democracy was condemned by all political theorists, and as an actual form of government it was unthinkable in England until much later. A modern-dress production divides the audience on party lines; the association of Coriolanus with a corrupt and defeated régime either undercuts the tragedy or perverts the spectators; and the saving graces of the hero—his courage, his unwillingness to play the hypocrite, his love for Virgilia—tend to be passed over. By inventing a spurious relevance the director hides the genuine and more universal relevance of the play.

When we are reading great literature of the past—*The Canterbury Tales* or *Paradise Lost*—or witnessing Elizabethan plays, we should not be thinking all the time of their relevance. We should rather by the exercise of imagination be partaking in the life of distant ages, and so extending our horizons and enlarging our sympathies. We ought as often to be aware of strangeness and difference as of resemblance and familiarity. Often, no doubt, there will be moments of recognition when, as Wordsworth said,

> in spite of difference of soil and climate, of language and manners, of laws and customs, in spite of things silently gone out of mind and things violently destroyed,

the literature of the past illuminates the present, so that we think not 'How unlike!' but 'How like . . .!' Such relevances, as Keats said of poetry, should 'appear almost a remembrance'. This provides a subtler pleasure than the kind of relevance which is obtained by obliterating temporal distinctions.

W. H. Auden, in his elegy on W. B. Yeats, remarked that

> The words of a dead man
> Are modified in the guts of the living.

We can never read a Jane Austen novel or a satire by Alexander Pope in the way their first readers did. We have different backgrounds, different educations, different literary experiences, somewhat different moral principles, and different sensibilities. With plays the obstacles to understanding are even greater: we can never hope—even in an exact replica of the Globe Theatre— to experience a play in the same way as the original audience did. The text, familiar to us, was not to them; our style of acting is different; our dramatic conventions have changed; our ideologies and superstitions are not the same as theirs; even our hygiene, our medicine, our dentistry, our diet, and our expectation of life are all different. However much, therefore, the director is anxious to bridge the gulf of the years, he will never wholly succeed; but he should try, at least, not to make the gulf wider.

It has been suggested above that the frantic pursuit of relevance limits the options. In other words, it forces one particular inter-pretation on an audience, when there are a number of others equally valid, and some less forced. Of course it may be argued that even before rehearsals begin any director must choose some options and reject others. We cannot have a neutral production,

and if we could it would be both confusing and dull. This point
has been put forcibly by Mr John Barton in an interview printed
in *Shakespeare Survey 25*:

> I think it's certainly impossible, and I question whether it's
> desirable. It's impossible because, as I've said, you have to be
> specific with actors. Actors have got to know what effect
> they're trying to make with a given line, what they mean and
> what they feel. When one reads the play in the study one can
> say again and again of a given line, 'I'm not sure what Shakes-
> peare intends here; it could be this or it could be that'. But
> however unsure one may be, one can't leave things uncertain
> for the actor; he has to be specific.

This does not quite answer the point; for, although Mr Barton
later admits that directors cannot completely control an audience's
response, he sums up his position by saying:

> I think the only point at which the play can be said to be
> absolutely open-ended is when it exists as a mere text waiting
> to be performed or studied.

To this one may ask: 'What if the fact that you are not certain of
Shakespeare's meaning is a sign not of some failure of expression,
or of comprehension, but, as Maurice Morgann suggested, of
deliberate ambiguity?' 'We have no right', he declared, 'to call
upon Shakespeare for explanations upon points which he means
to obscure.' The director can be entirely specific in his instruc-
tions to each of his actors, without necessarily jeopardizing the
freedom of interpretation of the play as a whole. He can say to his
Hamlet that 'Get thee to a nunnery' means what it says, or
alternatively 'Get thee to a brothel'. He can say 'Hamlet still loves
Ophelia' or 'He no longer loves her'. The words can be said sadly,
or bitterly, or savagely. But, in any case, the mystery of Hamlet's
character is still a matter for debate: a perfectly unambiguous
Hamlet would falsify the poet's meaning.

The point we are making can be clarified by two or three
examples. Stanley E. Hyman, in a recent book on Iago, shows that

a number of totally different interpretations can be squarely based
on the text of the play. Critics have traced his ancestry to the
devils of Moralities and Interludes; to Othello he is a demi-devil;
Iago himself refers to hellish theology—'divinity of hell'—and
compares himself to devils. Yet he may equally well be regarded
as a stage villain, as a follower of Machiavelli, as an unscrupulous
artist as Bradley, Swinburne, Hazlitt and others suggested and as
a latent homosexual. Oddly enough Mr Hyman does not mention
the two most obvious interpretations of the character's motives:
that he is professionally jealous of Cassio's promotion, and that he
was jealous of Emilia. Even the motivation provided by Cinthio—
that his love for Desdemona has been thwarted—finds some slight
support in the text, as when he confesses: 'Now I do love her too.'
The temptation facing a director is for him to choose one only of
these interpretations, and for him to instruct his actor accordingly.
Fresh from a study of Dr Leavis's essay, he may decide to treat
Iago merely as a stage villain; after reading S. L. Bethell or G. R.
Elliott, he will be driven to make him a devil, and he will be
deterred from making him Satan only by the knowledge that the
Prince of Darkness was a gentleman; after a diet of Freud and in
the post-Wolfenden climate he will make Iago a homosexual;
and, indeed, at the present day, he is likely to motivate his actions
by the colour of Othello's skin. It is surely apparent that a complete
commitment to any one of these interpretations would wreck the
play. If Iago is simply a devil, then the tragedy is reduced to a
Morality; if he is simply a stage villain, the play becomes a
melodrama; if he is simply a racialist, it becomes political proga-
ganda; and if he is a homosexual, it becomes a psychological
drama. Any of these directional choices would be an impoverishment of the play Shakespeare wrote, although the critics must
share the blame.

If we were to analyse the reactions of a member of an audience
to the delicate balance maintained in an uncommitted production
—one in which the director tried to keep the options open—we
should find that his attitude to Iago changed from scene to scene.
He would assume at the beginning that Iago's hatred of Othello
was caused by Cassio's promotion, though he would realize that

Iago was a hypocrite and a Machiavel. The words with which he rouses Brabantio might suggest to the spectator colour prejudice. In his soliloquy at the end of Act I, he reveals his fear of cuckoldry, and after framing his plot he invokes hell and night. In Act II he again reveals his jealousy, confesses his 'love' for Desdemona, and compares himself to devils. This ambiguity about his character will continue throughout the play until his very last words; and it is surely the duty of a director to preserve this ambiguity and not attempt to impose a clarity alien to Shakespearian dramaturgy. It is in pursuit of relevance that a director is most likely to sacrifice complexity; and there are apparently some dramatic critics who would prefer to witness a play on homosexuality or colour prejudice, and so be relieved of the tedium of unadulterated Shakespeare.

What has been said about Iago applies, to a lesser extent, to Othello, and to most of Shakespeare's major characters. Hamlet can be played in a variety of ways; but in whatever way it is played the audience should be given glimpses of the rejected ways. So with *Troilus and Cressida*. It has been interpreted as tragedy, comedy, tragical satire and comical satire; and whichever interpretation a director decides to adopt it is essential that the audience should be made aware of the discrepancies in the text which have led to such divergent opinions. There is the same problem with regard to *Measure for Measure*. Is the Duke a self-satisfied, blundering busybody, or a symbolic representation of God? Is Isabella a saint or a self-centred prig? Is the play a Christian parable on the necessity of forgiveness, or a satirical comment on the government of the universe? If the Director decides to make the Duke a symbol of 'power divine', we should not be prevented from laughing, with Lucio, at him; and if Isabella is presented as a saint, we ought nevertheless to recoil from her when she lashes out at the condemned Claudio. Or again, if *Troilus and Cressida* is presented as a comical satire, woe betide that director who will deny Troilus his moment of tragedy! In the great scene in Act V, where Troilus watches Cressida's swift infidelity, the point of view is continually changing; but the choric comments of Ulysses and Thersites—neither of them sympathetic characters—

ought not to do more than act as counterpoint to the agony of the hero.

Not one of Shakespeare's major characters can be summed up in a few sentences: they carry a penumbra of uncertainty. The sense we have of their truth to life is very largely due to the conflicting evidence we have of them—what is said of them, what they say themselves, the tension between theatrical convention and psychological realism. As Morgann pointed out, the greatest dramatists introduce an apparent incongruity of character, and Shakespeare was able to give life to his characters, partly because he lived in them, and partly because 'his mimic creation agrees in general so perfectly with that of nature'. This being so, an attempt to bring the plays up to date, and to make them relevant to the fashions of the day, upsets their metabolism. We do not need such desperate remedies; for even without them the plays continue to offer something fresh to each new generation. His profundity has been revealed little by little, and we may be sure that its depth is 'deeper than did ever plummet sound'.

III

Henry Vaughan's Ceremony of Innocence

A. J. SMITH

I

VAUGHAN'S *Silex Scintillans* draws much of its excited urgency
from the running attempt to come to terms with brutal and
scarcely intelligible events, with pain and afflictions which the
poet represents not merely as his private misfortunes but the stuff
of life as it unalterably is. From poem to poem there is a tussle,
immediate as the moment, between the felt sense of the experience
and the ability to comprehend, let alone resolve, the awful
difficulties, dilemmas, contradictions it may pose. Vaughan's
utterly uncertain grasp of his own poetic impulse is plain for all to
see, even in the stock anthology-pieces. Encountered in poem
after poem as one reads through the sequence there is certainly
something that needs accounting for in the unpredictable falterings
of power, whose effects are such as one might expect in a much
less considerable poet—too easy moralizings, mere compromises,
facile resolutions; marked disparities in the level of intensity and
seriousness; plain gaps between the raw confrontation and the
sense the poet can make of it.

Some such lapses may seem inevitable in an honest rendering
of so critical a struggle at the climax of a man's life, the price
his understanding must pay for the sheer intractable force with
which the issues come home. Possibly the poet endured—if
indeed he recognized them—some moments of lost insight as the
condition of his successes; and one must in any case ask oneself
why such moments are far more obvious in his poetry than they
would be in, say, that of Donne. Certainly there is no doubting
the sense of release and surge of powerful feeling when he finds
his way to an acceptable resolution, something that, working at

an adequate level of sensibility and understanding inseparably together, lifts his burden from him:

> O, is! but give wings to my fire,
> And hatch my soul, untill it fly
> Up where thou art, amongst thy tire
> Of Stars, above Infirmity;

('Disorder and frailty', lines 46–9)

Read cursorily or in snippets *Silex Scintillans* may impress more by its random glories than by a coherent pattern. But I think it must be seen in the first place—if only in the first place—as a whole, a continuing struggle to make sense of a few shattering experiences in a very few years of the poet's life, so that he may build anew. As a record of the shock to Anglican consciousness of the public events of 1648–9, and their consequences, the volume is a telling document in itself; but some private misfortune contingent upon the political and religious débâcle seems to have left the poet with the strong sense of a general cataclysm in which a man could only hope to save himself as best he might.

The anthology-poems, of course, give a very different impression of Vaughan; and it is a fair one as far as they go, for the ecstasies and the luminous images of an order beyond ours are important in his travail, though they are far from all that is there. But Vaughan's other-worldliness must not be misunderstood. In quite crucial ways it is the reverse of other-worldly. The poems themselves show that far from abandoning the natural order in favour of some disembodied state in the sky he was the more deeply committed to the life of nature by his apprehension of a world disintegrating about him and his sense that this could not be true reality. Vaughan took reality for man to be the first state of nature as God created it, which is not everywhere decayed even at this distance from the Fall; and he supposed that spiritual regeneration comes by way of a man's individual efforts to get back to that state:

Since then our businesse is, to rectifie
Nature, to what she was, . . .

(Donne, *To Sir Edward Herbert, at Julyers*, lines 33–4)

For some people in the seventeenth century, among them Vaughan's twin brother, 'rectifying nature' meant actual experiments with the supposed chemical properties of substances. Vaughan took the harder way of grappling with the frailties of our human apprehension itself. He set himself to acknowledge in full the conditions of our life in the fallen world and yet find in them the evidences of the final order of things. This resolve is plain to see in the poems themselves and has moral courage in a high degree. His purpose is not indeed to turn away from fallen nature but to search it the more intently for signs of its first state; not to flee in horror from the symptoms of our mortality but to confront them, even come to terms with them, if truth is to be found there.

It is clear that a family loss has much to do with the death-haunted mood of *Silex Scintillans* and is the most personal of the linked disasters that Vaughan confronts, for a sequence of poems which runs through both parts of the collection plots the course of his mourning over the event. One of these poems, 'Silence, and stealth of dayes!', written 'twelve hundred houres' after the death, speaks of the dead man as Vaughan's brother; and we now know in fact that there was a younger brother called William who died in 1648 at the age of twenty or so, perhaps of injuries sustained in the Royalist cause.[1] What distinctively matters for the poems is that the dead man was young, and therefore relatively uncorrupted by 'the world'; the poet's memories of him linger movingly on their childhood together and the death of innocence becomes a shaping preoccupation.

An untitled poem at the end of Part One of *Silex Scintillans*, 'I walkt the other day (to spend my hour)', marks a crisis in Vaughan's immediate attempts to accept the death[2]. There, in

[1] See F. E. Hutchinson, *Henry Vaughan*, Oxford, 1947, pp. 95–7 and 104–6.
[2] See my essay 'At the Grave of Henry Vaughan's Brother', *The Anglo-Welsh Review*, Spring 1967, pp. 31–42.

a telling figure, he digs the earth in winter to seek the buried life of a vanished flower and, uncovering it, learns suddenly that the flower will soon re-emerge 'most fair and young', having repaired 'Such losses as befel him in this air'. The new assurance turns back powerfully upon his own mourning:

> This past, I threw the Clothes quite o'r his head,
>   And stung with fear
> Of my own frailty dropt down many a tear
>   Upon his bed,
> Then sighing whisper'd, *Happy are the dead*!
>   *What peace doth now*
>   *Rock him asleep below*?

One cannot doubt that Vaughan has confronted his demon here and come to peace with it, welcoming his brother's early grave as itself providential. But the reconcilement, though decisive, is not quite final. One of the most beautiful pieces in *Silex Scintillans*, 'As time one day by me did pass', shows the poet still struggling some years later to settle his own response to the memory of the dead man. It is because that poem does move to a kind of finality that I attempt an exploratory reading of it below.

II

> As time one day by me did pass
>   Through a large dusky glasse
>   He held, I chanc'd to look
>   And spyed his curious book
> Of past days, where sad Heav'n did shed
> A mourning light upon the dead.

> Many disordered lives I saw
>   And foul records which thaw
>   My kinde eyes still, but in
>   A fair, white page of thin
> And ev'n, smooth lines, like the Suns rays,
> Thy name was writ, and all thy days.

O bright and happy Kalendar!
   Where youth shines like a star
   All pearl'd with tears, and may
   Teach age, *The Holy way*;
Where through thick pangs, high agonies
Faith into life breaks, and death dies.

As some meek *night-piece* which day quails,
   To candle-light unveils:
   So by one beamy line
   From thy bright lamp did shine,
In the same page thy humble grave
Set with green herbs, glad hopes and brave.

Here slept my thoughts dear mark! which dust
   Seem'd to devour, like rust;
   But dust (I did observe)
   By hiding doth preserve,
As we for long and sure recruits,
Candy with sugar our choice fruits.

O calm and sacred bed where lies
   In deaths dark mysteries
   A beauty far more bright
   Then the noons cloudless light
For whose dry dust green branches bud
And robes are bleach'd in the *Lambs* blood.

Sleep happy ashes! (blessed sleep!)
   While haplesse I still weep;
   Weep that I have out-liv'd
   My life, and unreliev'd
Must (soul-lesse shadow!) so live on,
Though life be dead, and my joys gone.

This poem appears in Part Two of *Silex Scintillans*, the set of
poems added when the volume was reissued in 1655, five years
after the first publication. It is evidently written later than those
occupied with the same event in Part One, for it looks back
elegiacally over a span of years to the death which the poems in

1650 had struggled to grasp. Yet it cannot be just the distance that makes this in every respect a better poem than most of those. Immediately preceding it in the 1655 section is 'The Seed growing secretly', which reduces to some banal moralizing one of Vaughan's most powerful ideas, death as an occult germination, by applying it to the poet's own retired life and refusal of worldly ambition. 'As time one day' shows an altogether finer order of imaginative life.

The poem opens with a curious figure, part allegory, part new science, as the manner of emblems was, which puts the chance recollection of some circumstances long past as a casual glance through Time's 'large dusky' perspective glass, disclosing Time's 'curious book/Of past days'. But far from fixing a cold general truth this emblem seizes a sudden self-realization which re-orders a man's sense of his whole life. Indeed what strikes one first is the way it focuses feeling, gathering the obscure impulses that attach to some stray thought which suddenly pulls one up with its neglected claim. Things already growing dim in the mind, a wan gleam in a cloudy past which persists in spite of one's will to have done with it—the elaborate scientific figure seems to be a way of getting at a peculiarly inward experience when it renders so precisely the sense of a distance from deeply mourned deaths, with all the accompanying charge of pain and guilt at the fading of recollection, the slackening of grief, the slipping out of mind of past love.

This opening figure is not developed as conceit or argument, for that is not the mode of the poem. Vaughan uses it to fix a perspective; his eye is on a state to be defined rather than an issue to be argued. So we move at once to what he saw as he glanced back through the dusky glass at his dead acquaintance; firstly, those 'disordered lives . . ./And foul records'

> which thaw
> My kinde eyes still . . .

Vaughan's control of a lyric movement is as subtly dramatic as Donne's or Herbert's but it works first to shape the voice of feeling. Here the relative 'which' picks out the comment almost as involuntary aside from the sad contemplation, giving the voice a sudden lift of passion that is wholly affecting. It is also a sudden lift of wit, which quietly suggests another kind of involvement with the fate of those dead acquaintances. His eyes thaw in 'kinde'-ness not only because their foul disordered lives have lost them to him forever, but because he too is human and weeps for his own mortality in them.

The complementary part of the vision stands against that first picture simply as another page in the book which is shown off by its opposite: 'Thy name' (presumably the dead brother's) and 'days' written in 'A fair, white page . . .' Again Vaughan does not build on the opposition or develop a dialectic out of it; his whole concern becomes the relation of his time-bound fleeting present to a resolved past. From the sharp stab of the voice over the disorderly lives one returns on a smooth descending cadence to the tranquil certainty the new image conveys, an assurance which may even seem overdone in the profusion of adjectives:

> fair, white page of thin
> And ev'n, smooth lines, like the Suns rays.

The heaped-up defining epithets do not add much to the force of the image. It is really the assured firmness of these emphases and the calm resolving force of the cadence itself that carries this mood off, giving the voice finality in the short line:

> Thy name was writ, and all thy days.

Now abruptly the narrative is quite arrested in a powerful new impulse. There is an outburst whose vehemence one might expect such a return to the past to provoke. But the voice modulates into unexpected celebration of a lost idyll of youth and innocence, a sudden blaze amid the images of dusk and gloom:

> O bright and happy Kalendar! . . .

Presented thus in the present tense the apparition has an immediacy beside which the rest of the poem seems pallid. Vaughan characteristically renders its forceful vitality in terms of heightened vision; and his diction suggests that this is a life we may see by looking into nature '. . . shines . . . star . . . pearl'd . . .' He offers us his sense of having got back to an absolute mark of his moral being, to find that it is not dimmed but enhanced and beautified by the distance and by his tears—whether they are those he shed then or those through which he views it now. Something seemingly dead has been recovered from the shrouding dark and found to live more intensely than before.

For the poet the revived private sentiment and the recovered truth are one. In mourning again he repossesses at least the sense of that state which age and conventional wisdom only heap dust on—innocent, vital, full of joy and love, the holy way because it points us to the nature of the creation itself. The simile of the tear-pearled star vividly fixes that fine complexity of feeling and attitude on which the whole poem turns. It shows loss, grief, distance, not annulled but transfigured into true life, and a saving sense of that life dependent upon our keeping keen the apprehension of such deaths.

Here one may see I think what the curious time-shifts of the poem amount to. They are meant to embody the pattern of a life. Vaughan moves back from the present to a centre of intense vital energy—the last moment of his true life—and then returns to the present with a sense of calm, distanced, resolution. The death marks precisely the term of his innocence and of youth's accompaniments of joy and spontaneous love. All he can do now is to see that event, and his subsequent life, in true perspective. So the poem turns upon a fixed truth which was there in the mind all the time but is now instantaneously recognized, as if given. There is no place here for the kind of urgent questioning one finds in Herbert. The splendid life of Vaughan's poem derives from his sense of the need to respond in the right way to a living universe, in which our own vitality has point while it is properly focused. He conceives of true life as a kind of concentrated power which our mortal nature only dissipates or smothers:

> Where through thick pangs, high agonies
> Faith into life breaks, and death dies.

Struggle, pain, then a violent bursting through and trampling down: the pangs and agonies of a young death are transformed into the positive energy of a heroic conquest over our resisting mortality.

He returns to the narrative movement quite insidiously through the long complicated analogy of the 'meek *night-piece*'. The *OED* cites these lines to illustrate a definition of *Night-piece* as 'A painting or picture representing a night-scene'; but Vaughan is evidently thinking of a trick effect in which something quite indecipherable in flat daylight shows up in clear relief when looked at in candle-light. The point here is that it is 'one beamy line' from the 'bright lamp' which displays the humble grave though day has 'quailed' it. He could not see the real sense of it *save* by looking back through the dusky light of time with the help of this one beam; not just when the death occurred, or shortly after, not even, perhaps, in the world's distracting daylight at all. Nor could the meaning of such a death be grasped without that shining of the star of youth—if one did not see youth as a mark like that, or the dead person's influence had not continued in its working, whether or not one regarded it:

> Gods Saints are shining lights . . .
> . . . these all night
> Like Candles, shed
> Their beams, and light
> Us into Bed.
>
> ('Joy of my life!', lines 17a and 21–4)

So there is a kind of final reckoning with the event, after years, in his confronting the grave now and in what its 'green herbs, glad hopes and brave' tell him. Those properties themselves prove powerfully equivocal. The death of youth and the consignment to dust of the great hopes one had for it, the mourning emblems strewn upon the grave, become the effective promises of new life, tokens of the glad hopes and brave assurances of resurrection and salvation. Vaughan keeps his two opposite motives quite precisely balanced in such images, suggesting that our grief and celebration are not in truth contraries.

But the poet seeks above all to make peace with himself for his dulled sense of the death:

> Here slept my thoughts dear mark! which dust
> Seem'd to devour, like rust;

The grave may be the 'dear mark' of his thought, an absolute trial of love, but it has none the less yielded to time and the inevitable effect of death itself which removes the object of love. Yet even death's dust, conceitedly, is other than it seems; time's thickening patina over the memory does not devour but preserves. The lines implicitly take up the sense of the opening image, the casual glance back and sudden shocked arrest which have led to this reliving the death. The lost life has been hidden, but it has emerged again at length in undiminished power and a clearer light.

III

One need not doubt that this is a decisive moment in *Silex Scintillans*. The poet has finally come to terms with his human frailty, whose most bitter symptom is the fading of the sense of shock and grief. So the sudden banality of his closing analogy momentarily disturbs one with the thought that his new truth may be too easily won when it needs to be confirmed in a conceited rationalization:

> As we for long and sure recruits,
> Candy with sugar our choice fruits.

Dust which preserves is another version of Vaughan's recurrent figure of occult incubation, the myth in which he casts his own retired existence; a buried virtue, transmuted, bursts forth in regenerated life. Plainly he wanted some image which would

not only tame his ghost by putting flesh back on it but show his
effective love paradoxically enhanced by distance and forgetfulness. 'Dust' brings some apt senses to bear but its preserving
powers do not seem equal to the task. And the matter-of-factness
of the writing becomes bathetic when 'preserve' hands him on to
candied fruit as a figure for the occult recruitment of choicest
beings, whose power endures the more certainly because the
'fruit' is thus sweetly hidden when it is just newly ripe. Vaughan
offers something to Johnsonian ideas of 'metaphysical' poetry
when he puts 'Candy with sugar' for dust, or for the effect of time,
distance, forgetfulness on the sense of shock and pain; though it is
plainly a deficiency of wit not an excess of it which trivializes
this thought. It says something for the way Vaughan's wit has
seemed to grasp his inner life that one's first reaction to a failed
conceit at this point is to doubt if the consoling triumph is wholly
justified after all.

What follows, though, is pure assurance, another sudden
arrest in the narrative movement to celebrate a moment picked
out of time. But now we are offered an image of luminous peace
rather than glorious vitality, a vision which accepts and transforms
the grave itself:

O calm and sacred bed . . .

Vision is important in the poem, as always in Vaughan, but the
vision is a way of saying something. The image in these lines
completes one's sense of looking at things that pass before the
eye casually as in an album, chance spots of brightness in the dusk
of time and consciousness. Here the flux itself is stilled and ordered.
The deathbed/grave is not—as youth is—caught in time and
receding with it, but fixed and final; it shows time itself to be
relative, as our mortal struggles and noon-days are relative to
such a calm refulgent dark. The quiet return to the present tense
catches anew this sense of order won out of chaos.

Yet the great beauty of the writing—horror transformed into
beauty—may not quite convince one that the final images of the
stanza grow out of the vision itself:

> For whose dry dust green branches bud
> And robes are bleach'd in the *Lambs* blood.

He writes '*For* whose . . .' not '*From* whose . . .'; but the connective can only be the idea of a transformation. The dry dust burgeons into regenerated life, the shroud becomes the immaculate dress of eternal life; one purity is transformed into another, vital innocence thus finally confirmed. These may be powerful ideas in themselves, and they are elaborated with succinct wit, but they seem to stand here as stuck-on consolations. The poem itself has not needed Christ's innocent blood so far; its casual introduction now suggests an uneasily divergent line of thought about death and salvation. The Atonement moves Vaughan powerfully elsewhere in *Silex Scintillans*, but what place does it have, save perhaps as one more instance, in his image of an occult incubation? The reticence of this belated appeal to Christ's absolving sacrifice suggests that Vaughan was not wholly sure how to reconcile his Christian convictions with the hermetic ideas that fed his imagination.

The benediction over the dead completes the poem by altogether turning the tables. It is the ashes which are happy in their assured sleep, the poet who is miserable. Vaughan's 'metaphysical' wit can be quite unlike that of Donne, or Herbert. The turn on 'weep' here is typical of the way he will unobtrusively draw successive meanings out of the same gesture, as though reading deeper in the universal order itself. One understands him to mean firstly that it is only the survivors who weep while the dead man himself is in bliss; knowing this, we may yet have to weep in mortal frailty because we cannot see beyond the temporary loss. But then the impulse returns upon itself. His tears are truly justified after all; not now because his brother has died, or because he too must die and laments his own death in another's, or even by his earlier forgetfulness of the death—but just because he himself still lives. The poem asks us to take that avowal in both a private and a general sense, as expressing at once the emptiness of his life now his brother is dead, and the recognition that having outlived his youth and innocence he himself is the true corpse.

Here at any rate the effect is finely brought off, in a perfect closure of cadence and complex sense. One need not have followed through *Silex Scintillans* the years of wrestling with this difficulty to feel the force of a resolution which finally gets the poet's relation to the obliterating passage of time into true perspective— indeed, puts time itself in its place. The event stands outside time, and is not destroyed if all awareness of it fades; on the contrary, it negates time by showing time's pointlessness. Starting out to mourn the death, he has found more bitter cause to mourn in the way time dims the shock and even memory of it; and he finishes now by mourning that survival which leaves him caught up in time and vulnerable to its effects. So the large image of the poem is turned, too. The discomforting vision of something receding into the past, towards oblivion, assumes a different if no less disturbing aspect. Such virtues stay and shine, an absolute mark; it is we survivors who move on in oblivious unreality.

Vaughan has the 'metaphysical' ability to sustain an intricate thought through a tense lyric movement; but the marvellous rightness of the last stanza has to do with the delicate inflections of voice and mood within the fine arch of the cadence, the sense of a perfected gesture. One might speak of an affective rhetoric; but the effect of the precise phrasing and varied repetition is really to articulate both mood and idea as one response, to shape and intensify the passion by completing the thought. The idea develops with the shifting voice of feeling, or seems to be con- trolling it, which is why the mood itself can modulate so subtly— and so unsentimentally, too. The resolution emerges in the emphatic poise and counterpoise of the last line with a feel of definitiveness: '. . . life . . . dēad/ . . . mȳ jōys gőne'—the sudden acceleration and last extra emphasis closing the movement, emptying the sense, confirming a finality which is not merely that of the poem.

This is a lyric poem which gets much of the beauty of its effect and movement from such sensitively modulated shifts of address and mood in a powerful dramatic logic. Like a Shakes- peare soliloquy or a Romantic symphony it works its way through a whole cycle of vivid attitudes: forgetful calm, effort and struggling, intense contemplation, moved and wondering celebration, final valediction and the full self-realization which makes the closure possible. In following out that inner process, with all its inflections of point and feeling, one has the sense of sharing a ritual, a completed movement of the mind and spirit which has general truth. Vaughan's poem is a little drama in itself, not least in the way it stands so decisively between the past and the future. Above all, the poem has that organic wholeness of vision one looks for in true art in which form, movement and effects are all integral to the sense. Its complex life renders the apprehension so powerfully, and inevitably, that one seems to see the movement of the mind itself.

IV

Vaughan only rarely manages so entire an integration of the imaginative and intellectual life of a poem; but I suppose that no one who reads this piece attentively would want to endorse A. Alverez's comment: 'I am not sure that, by the standards of Donne and Herbert, Vaughan was ever able to think at all'.[1] If Vaughan did not think like Donne or Herbert or Marvell (as they did not think like each other) it is partly because he was responding to the pressures of his own time and circumstances with his own distinctive apprehension of the universe we live and die in. *Silex Scintillans*, like Dante's *Vita Nuova*, is a climactic utterance, the poetry of a man who has just been born anew; it begins with a poem called 'Regeneration'. But unlike Dante, Vaughan has to struggle to confirm his vision in a world which apparently denies it; and his mature poems are a series of fervent attempts to get past the dust of our own mortality to the covert reality which we can no longer directly apprehend, and which will disclose itself only to the truly regenerate:

> Onely this Veyle which thou hast broke,
> And must be broken yet in me, . . .

('Cock-crowing', lines 37–8)

[1] *The School of Donne*, 1961, p. 89.

The universe Vaughan inhabits is the antithesis of Newton's because he conceived that it is not inert but essentially alive, not neutral but purposeful—animated by joy and love, and providentially disposed for our good. So he seizes on the vitality of the natural creation as the principle of its moral life, attempting repeatedly to render it in images of energy, light, focused power, magnetic force. To be open to these powers working around us is to recover as much as we now can of the condition of the early men, those who had familiar commerce with God's agents such as the Old Testament describes—'An Angell talking with a man' ('Religion', line 4). Announcing himself on the title-page of the first *Silex Scintillans* as 'Henry Vaughan *Silurist*' the poet marks together his local allegiance, and his moral progress (which is a regress in time). But at this distance from the Fall even the regenerate man must find what universal truth he can in the hieroglyphic sign of it that each created thing bears as the mark of its own purpose; and Vaughan looks for these signs in the peculiar life of nature which surrounds him:

All things here shew him heaven; *Waters* that fall
Chide, and fly up; *Mists* of corruptest fome
Quit their first beds and mount; trees, herbs, flowres, all
Strive upwards stil . . .

('The Tempest', lines 25–8)

What denies the vital coherence of the universe, or masks it from us, cannot itself be a force of life. Vaughan consistently speaks of sin as a disintegration into dust or a blinding with dust, that dust which is all we corrupted beings see when we look at our world now and accept it for our only reality:

O knit me, that am crumbled dust! . . .
The world
Is full of voices; Man is call'd, and hurl'd
By each, he answers all, . . .

('Distraction', lines 1 and 11–13)

To share that condition of random distractions and dispersals is to define ourselves as dust before our bodily death.

In the seventeenth century plenty of people shared Vaughan's belief in an animate universe of fixed qualities, providentially ordered. These long-dead ideas have life and truth in him because they serve his imaginative grasp of his own, and our, experience. He is a 'metaphysical' poet in that he saw universal processes at work in natural events and apprehended both orders simultaneously, and with equal force:

> Man is one world, and hath
> Another to attend him.
>
> (Herbert, 'Man', lines 47–8)

So Vaughan wrote poems that live, while his twin brother sought his spiritual renewal in futile alchemical experiments. The poems in *Silex Scintillans* draw much of their distinctive character from Vaughan's strivings to live out, imaginatively and intellectually, a felt metaphysic. Many of them are direct attempts to seize some distinctive activity of nature and to read its special quality as a divine hieroglyph; though such poems tend to be inherently unbalanced precisely because the force of the realization necessarily matters so much more to him than his all too human fumblings after its 'meaning'. The ejaculatory suddenness, the vehemence, express another mode of the intense will to believe that reality is there in the natural manifestation, just beyond dust-clouded eyes, to be won by the force of a spiritual resolve or to take one aback with a momentary gleam of its naked splendour. Vaughan is committed to visual projections in a way that no other 'metaphysical' poet was because he conceived that reality is accessible to us as something immediately seen, a momentary piercing of the dust and dark.

He was committed as fervently to a few drastic impulses and affections, whose quality he urgently tries as a measure of his regenerate prowess. His poems show him striving to open himself to the vital forces at work in the natural creation, and especially to sympathize with and participate in the universal impulses of joy and of love:

> O Joyes! Infinite sweetnes! with what flowres,
> And shoots of glory, my soul breakes, and buds!
>
> ('The Morning-watch', lines 1–2)

So he may strike one as a poet of extremes of feeling—gloom and radiance, despair and utter certitude, savagery and tender compassion. Despite the fierce bitterness of his animadversions on his times and the people who controlled them he has a more sensitive humanity than most in that age, a finer sense alike of human vulnerability and of human dignity. 'As time one day' grows out of his grasp of a frailty which has dimmed the power of naked human love. The sudden chance thought of his neglected love for his dead brother, putting such vivid pictures before the mind, becomes in itself providential. The seed has grown secretly; something long buried in the memory has germinated there and can now emerge as a resolved truth.

It is especially striking that a thought of lost childhood at once focuses Vaughan's most powerful impulses. Here, as in a few other places, two strong motives come together—the sense of personal loss and desolation, and the belief that innocence dies with childhood. So he laments at once the loss of a childhood companion, the loss of his own childhood, and the loss of innocence; and his conceit that death and the grave are a glorious recovery of loss makes the poem so powerfully moving, as well as definitive. A retreat, if one could manage it, would be another way, leading perhaps to an actual recovery of innocence. But here the retreat of memory points only to the grave and leaves the present life a shadowy, pointless interim. One remarks how much deeper that thought goes in the seventeenth-century poet than in the modern mourner, however intensely someone might now apprehend a private loss.

What did Vaughan make of his life in the forty-odd years of it left to him after he published the enlarged *Silex Scintillans*? Nothing he wrote thereafter suggests that he did more than follow out the acceptance attained in this poem. But to think of that retirement as a calm won out of passion is to recognize that such poetry as Vaughan's is not born of emotion recollected in tranquillity. On the contrary, it is itself active experience, an engagement of the whole consciousness such as properly deserves the name of thought. The shift from a lyric poetry conceived as immediate experience to poetry which recollects or reflects upon experience has much to do with the difference between Vaughan and, say, Keble.

The Prison Manuscripts of William Combe

COLIN FRANKLIN

As THE possession and familiar company of manuscripts may offer a special form of acquaintance with their author, it seems appropriate to write about William Combe who is best remembered as poet of Doctor Syntax. Collections of his papers exist where one would expect to find them but most of the work he did for Ackermann, and to provide text for Rowlandson's aquatint illustrations, is in two folio volumes which Professor Harlan Hamilton calls the Fleming Papers. These have now come back to England from New York and are the subject of this essay.

The last quarter-century of Combe's long life was spent in King's Bench prison as a busy scribbling debtor, and during it he made the reputation which lives. Before, he had written satirical or political books and became editor of *The Times*; after, he was associated with the most enterprising publisher in the visual history of books. As Professor Hamilton says in his biography,

> For the rest of his life Combe was to be engaged in this kind of journeyman work, writing prose and verse to accompany aquatints, chiefly those turned out by Ackermann's staff of engravers and colourists. The books produced by this collaboration include many items highly prized by collectors today: *History of Westminster Abbey* (1812), *Antiquities* of York (1813), *Poetical Sketches of Scarborough* (1813), the histories of *Oxford* (1814), *Cambridge* (1815), the *Colleges* (1816), *Madeira* (1821), and most important of all his work with Rowlandson, the three *Tours of Doctor Syntax* (1812, 1820, 1821), the *Dance of Death* (1815, 1816), the *Dance of Life* (1817), and *Johnny Quae Genus* (1822). During these years he also produced similar books for other publishers, including *The Thames, or Graphic Illustrations*

(1811), *Picturesque Views on the Southern Coast* (1826), and *Pompeii* (1827).

The two folio volumes, with manuscript of almost all the books in Professor Hamilton's paragraph, belong to his prison years. These are the pages covered in confinement, living in discipline, working and earning; but the sacramental character of such a manuscript rests in the presence there of the man himself. Here is old Combe, doggerel to the left of a sheet and rough accounts in space on the right—'Mrs R, £13—, Hair—6', and (a large bill) 'Butcher 4–17–10½'. Or beyond his verse frontier come draft petitions to the Prince, blurbs for Ackermann, letters to his friend Maria Brooks. Some are out of order, upside-down, verses over the faded ink of his history of an Oxford college.

An early note, from bookseller or auctioneer no doubt, is bound into the beginning:

Combe's (Dr) Manuscripts in one thick folio volume containing the originals of Dr. Syntax, Quae Genus, Accounts of Public Edifices & Schools, the University of Oxford, various Histories of Towns, Essays, Poems, Works written for professed Authors who could not write themselves, a curious defence written in the name of the Marshal of the King's Bench concerning his Conduct in connection with Lord Cochrane's escape & giving several curious particulars of the circumstances attending the same, and many other things altogether a very interesting volume but in sad confusion having been very badly used by the Doctor himself who wrote just where the book opened, either end upwards very imperfect—many places the original manuscript has been covered by a second composition being written over it with a coarse pen.

This eloquent paragraph suggests the charm of Combe's manuscript, and quality of his life ('either end upwards very imperfect'). Though their early history is unknown, a letter from his bigamous and estranged wife Charlotte to Ackermann, soon after Combe's death, records the existence of manuscripts which may well be these. Unhappily she cannot manage to pay his debts unless the M.S. Papers which you kindly Collected and which are in Mrs Ryves's hands should prove deserving your acceptance.—Anthony mentions that you thought some were of value. I have the smallest Idea what they contain, and therefore you are the best judge if they are worth more than the £90—due to Mrs R—I can only say that I should be most happy could I present them to you *unincombered* by so havey a Debt—

As they are his chief work from the prison decades, it seems unlikely any other late gathering of Combe's manuscripts would then have been reckoned 'of value'. In the author's hand a preliminary page is headed 'K. Acquaintance with Ackerman 1809'. Combe in his writing used K to stand for King's Bench. It seems they came to Ackermann in one folio volume but late in the nineteenth century somebody bound the collection handsomely in two, contriving to gild the edges without damaging text.

One fascination of Combe's chaos was his pursuit of literary success in the King's Bench prison, and preservation of self-respect. As a hack his position appears in some pride of definition. 'For my ordinary drudgery', he tells one correspondent for whom he has worked, 'I shall be paid my ordinary price'. Upside down in the middle of an account of Switzerland, upon the top of other matters, appears an uncompleted thought,

> But whatsoe'er may be the station
> Where chance may find my next vocation—

This was his station—hack, professional writer, freelance. On the right of *Quae Genus* verses he gives out of the blue a list of work he can recall over the years, including

Not less than 2,000 columns in Newspapers.—The minor contributions I do not presume to number—Memoranda of 64 memorials to different boards, &c. for various Applicants— 73 Manuscript Sermons, some of which were published—

Then he wanders to the Ackermann years of steadier work and a prison home:

Various Assistances in verse in his poetical Magazine; as illustrations of its plates. For several years a monthly Contributor to Ackermann's literary repository—The Female Tatler, through several years of monthly continuation; but in them I had frequent assistant contribution.

The manuscripts show how Ackermann called upon his help for the minor chores which now belong to a publicity staff. The painting and construction of carriages interested Ackermann all his days, so when a book on the theme is ready Combe provides its advertisement. The ingenious publisher had invented and patented a kind of movable axle. 'The Utility derivable from building carriages with these Axles' he has to grind out, 'or adding them to old ones it is confidently presumed will be proved to the satisfaction of every one who will favour this work partial attention —' A subscription list is needed for a proposed publication, following the success of his *Oxford* and *Cambridge*—a *History of the Colleges*, the work now known as 'Ackermann's Public Schools'; so Combe drafts a form of appeal to the public. A prefatory note for the Third Tour of Doctor Syntax is scribbled, and a blurb for the newly completed *Dance of Life*. Princess Charlotte has died, Ackermann issues prints of her; subscriptions are invited, so Combe prepares the notice. He gives also an example of poems to be provided with them—'illustrations of its plates', in his own humble phrase. As poet this lay some way from his line of country:

O much lov'd Princess, o'er thy dear remains
Music laments in unavailing strains
Through Death's long night. Faith sheds her cheering ray
And light the passage to eternal day.

Though writing to order can never have been as simple as it seems, Combe in old age came near the end of invention and we find him drafting a letter to a lady, when the *Dance of Life* was on, at a loss for situation or episode to illustrate Rowlandson:

I am rather flattered that you should think the Dance of Death to be a superior production in point of Composition to

Dr. Syntax:—because that opinion is my own;—& it has occurred to me to form a work as a companion to it, to be named the Dance of Life. Now, most excellent Lady, will you either beneath a Laurel or at your own table, or in your dressing Room, will you beckon a Muse to come to you— There are seasons when the Plough-share is still; when the activity of vegetation is silent, & Labour enjoying the comparative Indolence of Expectation. You might then vary, or rather occupy the Scene, by calling into activity the extra-ordinary powers you possess in the way which I propose—If they were only your first thoughts I would thank you for them (In any verse, in any measure)—The secret is now out:—I shall say no more (on the subject).

The old bookseller's description of the manuscript is pleasantly true of some parts. Passages of *Quae Genus* come over the top of Combe's account of Merton College for Ackermann.

> And in the scramble on the table
> He got as much as he was able

we learn, reading between the lines. Notes about Queen's College appear on the back of a cutting about racing at Newmarket, from the *Sporting Intelligence* of 1808—so helping to date the early pages of these volumes. They live as a study of method, Combe's working day.

Other aspects of Ackermann's enterprise also needed Combe's help. Though we remember him for aquatint, he was early in England to use lithography—a friend of Senefelder its inventor, issuing examples of the new method in his *Repository of the Arts* and bringing out the English version of Senefelder's book in 1818. The public had to be aware of such development. A tax on lithographic stone was proposed, and Combe drafts with some labour and correction a rather specious argument against it. His draft is literally transcribed:

A Motion having been made in Parliament to introduce a Bill for the purpose of imposing a Duty on Calcareous Stones employed in the Art of Lithography now introduced into this Country, and which promises a new feature in the Arts hitherto unknown or which has not been practised in GB I beg to leave submit to your consideration such reasons as my extensive experience suggests me on a subject in which the fine Arts and a very considerable branch of trade are materially interested. Lithography, though well known, as it is most extensively to the very great Advantage of the places where it has been more particularly cultivated and encouraged—It is however but new in this country, though if cultivated and encouraged promises uncommon improvement in a branch of the fine Arts, which have taken such a deep root in the British Soil, and form such beneficial article in the trade of it.

It is a commercial principle founded in a just sense of public Interest & political Justice, that new Inventions should ever be nourished and protected:—in order to raise them into that Importance, Stability and general adoption which may allow for their extensive circulation of being subject to future Taxation.—The Species of Stone which is proposed to be Taxed is to be found in England but by no means of a quality sufficient to allow of execution equal to that brought from Germany, and the latter is brought 1000 miles, from the interior of that Country, and so great an expence, that any Tax made payable thereon would amount to a Prohibition.— Besides the Quantity imported would be comparatively so small, that it could not be worth the attention of Government to impose it. Indeed it would appear to be a wiser rather to propose a bounty to encourage their—

Two pages later he prepares a letter, to the Society of Arts, which will go with a copy of Senefelder's book and canvass its suitability for a reward the Society has offered 'for the improvement of this among other important discoveries'. Publicity on behalf of new discovery could not have come easily to Combe in his eightieth year; but he could generally call upon Ackermann for money, and the charge was reversed for these occasional chores.

As comic poet, Combe's position remains a strange one and his method unaccountable. For years he never spoke with Rowlandson, but in some partnership of temperament invented his long verse episodes as text for the drawings which arrived. From accident, it seems to have become a condition of work. To advertise the *Dance of Life* he drafts a note, explaining that if 'a more intimate connection has taken place between the Artist and the writer, the same principle has in a great measure if not altogether predominated in the structure of this composition, as in that of the Tour of Dr Syntax & the Dance of Death'.

Though it would be foolish to examine the manuscripts in thesis-detail for working method, ample evidence is there. He seems to have written fluently, almost in a coma once the flow started. There are changes, afterthoughts and deletions of course, but in thousands of lines relatively few. An oddity of the *Second Tour* of Doctor Syntax is the tiresome length of obituary at the start, for his stupid wife Dolly who had been an entertaining figure of ridicule while she lived. It is therefore of some interest to observe that Combe wrote these passages emotionally, with more care and correction than most of his verse received, some passages transposed, new ink and handwriting as of a long session ended and a fresh start when she is truly dead.

One follows the progress of his Madeira book through that Regency mixture of third-hand history and foolish doggerel at the service of entirely charming art. The faithful and famous account of a Skimmington ride, as Syntax observes the procession of Yorkshire villagers teasing the life out of a man who lets himself be too much bullied by his wife, is here—and the touching visit of Syntax to Nimrod, old Apperley the sporting writer, for which Combe makes notes of a few likely dog names before using them in his verse lines. And there is the pleasure of finding first drafts of successful passages from several of the books—as for instance the embarrassment of Sir Henry in the *Dance of Life*, when he confesses financial trouble which rules out the new barouche on which his wife had set her hopes. This differs slightly from the published version:

> As for Barouches, be it known
> I soon, dear girl, may sell my own.

There's a sad rent in my affairs,
But you I know will sooth my cares!
Though the world frowns you will beguile
My downcast spirits with a smile,
Now till this cloud is past and over
We both must cease to live in clover
In humble style you'll be content,—
Besides you have your settlement
When redd'ning up she fiercely said,
And *I know too, if 'tis not paid*
That you in *Limbo* shall be laid,
The contest warmd and words arose
Which I shall leave to vulgar prose,
My Muse is chaste nor would rehearse
The criminating slang in verse.
But she will tell with vixen grace,
Miss threw the coffee in his face,
And in her passion's wild Uproar
Dash'd all the Crock'ry on the floor,
And spurn'd him, in the way of trade,
From out the House for which He paid.

It would be absurd to search Combe's on-demand writing for news about his private life, though the deep irony in the characterization of Vellum, the bookseller, comes undisguised from memory. In such a scattering of notes and drafts from a working life spent in King's Bench prison, hints and points of view abound.

The years never diminished his pleasure in mild intrigue or playful exchange with women. He must have been in correspondence, as we know he was at dinner parties, a charming but unscrupulous friend. Here in old age is his Valentine to Miss S— W—:

While I behold her animated Face
Her gentle goodness and her native grace
Her early mind each well-trac'd charm receives
From the example which a mother gives.
Take then the praise sincere for such is mine.
Thus sings her faithful, grey-hair'd Valentine.

And shall I now awake the untuneful String
Strain my weak voice and in my winter sing
But you inspire and will accept the Lays
That fond Affection to her virtue pays.

This was unexceptionable, but Combe's life had more puzzling troubles. After the insanity of his first wife he tended to ignore the wretched connection and married Richard Cosway's sister-in-law Charlotte. When that failed and she crossed to Ireland he formed friendships of inconstant strength and seriousness of purpose. The manuscripts are scattered with ample evidence in letters, verse or long complaint. One of his last and strangest books, the collection of letters to Maria Brooks, took its course over this period and near the end he asks for their return, having publication in mind. One long draft letter, an apology and explanation for eloping, must have been written (like so much of his work) to solve the distress of another life. Combe became a kind of third-party insurance premium.

It is therefore the more moving when a different voice speaks and one hears him for a moment, for we have listened to chatter and missed the man. After harsh words about a poem submitted for his criticism, he goes on (transcribed literally):

And now for your important Questions.—I am not happy for I am a human being to whom happiness is not a natural & therefore not a possible possession: but I am perfectly content, and therefore so happy as I can, or ought to be.—Death never was an object of terror, in the gaieties, pleasures and splendor and sad meridian of Life. Nor am I now, when I am now when in two months I shall attained 76 Years, and am in the near neighbourhood of his Domain.—I never could think death an Evil, because it is universal; and an universal evil, cannot be the work of all good, just & merciful Being, who made us subject to it.—Life has ever appeared to me as a probationary State, I cannot reconcile it to reason under any other character, a future being must follow it—Besides, the belief of another Life, is a belief as universal as Life itself:—and he who made man would not have inspired with this Idea, wherever he lives & breathes,

if it had not been among the Decrees of Heaven:—Besides, I
have an internal conviction, an inexplicable conscience, superior
to all reason, from the contemplation of my own frame & the
powers that direct & govern, that I have an immortal spirit
within me. Our nature is combination of the Brute and the
Angel.—when the former perishes, the latter gains its freedom
& is itself again.

Artistic judgment appears in these drafts of letters and articles—
upon Lord Byron for instance, and the Royal Academy about
which he is amusingly satirical:

It still continues to be, in a predominant measure, a collection
of portraits, and a Stranger might be led to suppose from a view
of it, that the English people preferred as pictures the faces of
their Friends or their own to any other subjects.

He admires 'Sir James Lawrence' and praises Turner in so far as he
imitated Claude Lorrain, but cannot digest his unorthodox
treatment of a sky, 'the sole defect in this magnificent Landscape'.
As for architecture, a few notes towards an essay express impec-
cable principles: 'There are those who mistake whim for Genius
and ornament for taste. Use is the first object,—& then beauty
follows'.

So he lived, using a moderately comfortable room in the 'State
House', the privileged part of the prison, as his working study;
dining out with Walter of *The Times* or with Ackermann's
family, visiting the Academy and taking long country walks.
Debtor's prison, for such as he or Leigh Hunt, seems to have been
viewed with absolute tolerance in social courtesy. At Combe's
time of life the place may have looked to him and others as we
perhaps see an Old People's Home, and he as a guest suffered no
more embarrassment than a visitor now from any comparable
institution. His own view of King's Bench confirms this, and
appears clearly more than once. He had worked it out, or accepted
it, and one must be impressed by the sensitivity of the time which
digested such an attitude towards debt and among debtors. Their

creditors may have felt otherwise, but anger was pointless and the prison notion came nearer to therapy than revenge:

> Imprisonment is not to be considered as a state of Punishment, but as a provisional Security of the Debtors person, of which the Creditor has thought proper to take possession, till the debt is paid or such other compensation is made, as shall satisfy the Creditor. And if it appears that such security is amply guaranteed by the Rules as by the enclosures, it does not appear that the C[reditor] sustains any injury, by their being allowed to remain, as they have been immemorially established.

> One of the great distresses and injurious results to debtors, who have a prospect of settling with their Creditors, or a wish by personal Exertions and oeconomical Habits to attain that object, is a separation from their families, which is prevented by the means which the R[ules] afford of preventing such a disunion . . .

> Why are not debtors who are among the superior ranks of Life, for such there are, to be allowed indulgences suited to their habits of their situation & education, provided those Indulgences do not lessen the security which the C^r claims from the walls of a Prison . . .

Long passages of the manuscripts describe and defend the reasonable living condition of imprisoned debtors. As there is no room to quote these at length, one may simply note their agreeable cause; for it seems the Marshall of the King's Bench needed to defend himself against serious criticism in these matters, after Lord Cochrane had made his escape and so called the whole system into question. Combe was writing on the Marshall's behalf. What more natural and sensible than to engage a debtor so experienced in presenting the troubles of others as if they were his own, to defend the prison system? Especially when his own privilege might be under fire. It was the strangest writing commission in Combe's long service life.

On the whole, having partly overcome or denied the humiliation, his prison years were the best he knew—having no taste for common dissipation (always a water-drinker) or for travelling in the places he fluently described; not needing family life because so thoroughly failing in that direction, but free to wander, visit, dine and receive. In one prison episode we see him most clearly, for Combe was driven mad by noisy children and nothing so defines the life of a man as its minor irritants. Rowlandson's aquatint of the prison in Ackermann's *Microcosm of London* shows where Combe's rooms were, in the State House, over-looking the outside world; but below him younger prisoners played in the rackets court, and children then as now loved to shout their support or comment upon a game. Combe found this such a penetrating nuisance that 'racket' must have taken new meaning there. His complaints to authority, pained and restrained, on this theme are nearer the true voice of feeling than most of what he wrote—and show him, struggling against adversity in his room, the elderly artist unable to defeat distraction.

I am not going to make a charge against the general conduct of the children within the walls—that is an evil which must in time cure itself—but against one particular Item of it, of which I feel the hourly annoyance.—On the racket Grounds beneath my window, Children are employed by the Racket Masters, as it is called, to cry the Game:—of which I can give you a very clear Idea by supposing, a Chimney Sweeper, a Sprat woman, or any person engaging in those vociferating occupations, were to be crying their respective trades under your window.—I say nothing upon the effect of bringing up children in this way,—that is not the worst way in which these unhappy Urchins are brought up in this place. My complaint is that such a noise is made by them, who have no right to be in the place, to the disturbance of those who are compelled to be there.—But it appears to me, that the Racket Masters, are the Masters of the Place, and the Protectors of the Children in all their noise, riotous behaviour & impudence, in defiance of any orders of Yours.—I have complained frequently to Mr. Morris,—and he has promised that I should hear no more of it:—but his remonstrance is treated with contempt, and I have been personally insulted in consequence of it,—and the other evening I was saluted with the title of the Bloody old Thief, who wanted to turn out the Boys.—At this very moment ½ past 8,—seven Boys are playing at Rackets with much hallooing &c—under

my window & some of them have been so engaged since seven
o Clock of which event the Watchman must know; who, if he
did his Duty should inform You. But this by the way,—the
subject of my complaint, is the crying the Game by these
unhappy Boys, Mr. Morris if you think proper, will explain it;
as I have pointed it out to him while he has been in my room.—
It strikes every visitor of mine, as an intolerable evil,—it has
always been bad, but it is now become worse than ever; and as
the days are getting long, & I shall probably continue here, if I
live, through the Summer, I trouble you with the hope, that
your officers will receive such directions, as you may think
proper to relieve me from the useless and idle Interruptions of
which I have been compelled to complain; and which will, in
fact be beneficial to the Children whose injurious Occupation I
wish to interrupt.

It is one of several similar preparations; laced with a little
special-pleading, when he suggests the boys will themselves be
better off if rescued from their 'injurious' but obviously happy
'crying of the game'. This was his way, as when he pleaded for
Ackermann against a tax on lithographic stones, that their present
return was not yet ripe for swingeing revenue if such were
imposed.

Yet he provides a living self-portrait from that evening of early
summer in King's Bench prison; the Bloody old Thief writing in
his three-quarters filled-up pages, terribly distracted but making
prose which is forever Combe, not playing arpeggios for the
solo artist.

V

'Brother Wearers of Motley'[1]

[To the memory of Geoffrey Tillotson and Henri A. Talon,
two great critics prematurely lost to Thackeray studies]

SYLVÈRE MONOD

HAVING for many years conducted studies of the author-reader relationship in the works of several Victorian novelists, I had long felt that Thackeray posed more problems, and problems of a more daunting complexity, than his contemporaries. But that is all the more reason for eventually coming to grips with them. The choice of *Pendennis* and *Esmond* for such a purpose may seem arbitrary and therefore requiring justification. Why not a single novel, and why not *Vanity Fair*? Because there has been no dearth of adequate criticism of *Vanity Fair*. Because it was Thackeray's first truly great novel, and it is usually even more interesting to examine a novelist's *second* major work, always revealing and often decisive. Because *Pendennis* appears at first sight to justify the strictures of traditional Thackerayan criticism. Because *Esmond*, while very close to its immediate predecessor in time, was yet antithetical to it in craftsmanship.[2] And because the years 1849–52 thus provide an exceptional vantage-point from which to study Thackeray's creativity.

To deal with all the aspects of two huge novels—some 1,500 pages in all—having some relevance to the relationships studied

---

[1] Thus are Thackeray's readers apostrophized by the narrator of *Vanity Fair* (Chapter XIX). Since no standard edition of Thackeray's works is available, references are to chapter-numbers only (or, for *Esmond*, to book- and chapter-numbers), given in the text of the article.

[2] Of *Esmond*, George Saintsbury writes: 'it is certain that, great as are its parts, the whole is greater than almost any one of them—which is certainly not the case of *Pendennis*' (Introduction to Oxford edition of Thackeray's works, 1908; reprinted in *The History of Henry Esmond*, ed. T. C. & W. Snow, 1909, p. xiii).

here would require a book-length essay rather than a mere article. This is therefore more in the nature of an outline and an interim statement than an exhaustive treatment of the theme.

I

Thackeray's choice of narrators and his use of them are governed by two major urges, which are mutually contradictory. On the face of it, he would seem to have been reluctant to speak in his own name, at least in his fiction. *Pendennis* is supposedly written by an anonymous, rather shadowy person, of whom we know little enough except that he is not Thackeray himself or Arthur Pendennis, though he is the latter's friend as well as the 'chronicler' of his 'history'. Henry Esmond is, of course, the narrator of his own adventures. Arthur Pendennis is, more surprisingly, the narrator of *The Newcomes* and *The Adventures of Philip*—surprisingly because he had begun life as a novelist of some promise, not a mere historian of his friends' lives. Of course, every novelist, as has been shown more than once, uses a narrator, a narrating *persona* distinct from his own private personality even when he does not specify that individual's identity and characteristics. But Thackeray's case is peculiar in that he likes, and almost seems to need, to dissociate himself from his narrators explicitly. This is no doubt connected with his well-known love of disguise and pseudonymous signatures. It had been useful to him in his early parodies, but it also corresponded to a deeper impulse in his literary personality, of which it formed the more reticent side. Writing as Esmond or Pendennis or George Warrington—in the last quarter of *The Virginians*—was no doubt more artistically ambitious than, but not essentially different from, writing as Barry Lyndon or James Yellowplush.

Yet, no less of course, a man does not write in order to remain hidden. He writes in order to express himself. By publishing a book he makes himself public. And the urge to confess himself in public was certainly just as potent in Thackeray as the urge to disguise himself—the latter, indeed, acting only as a restraint on the former. By using a first person that is distinct both from himself and from his central character, he plays on both sides: his first-person narrator inevitably keeps in touch with the author, but is at the same time someone else for whom he is not outwardly responsible, whom he may often explicitly repudiate and occasionally satirize. To a man of Thackeray's temperament, disguise in a way facilitates self-revelation by making it less perilous, less exposed, and by rendering it permanently ambiguous. Thackeray's relationship with the narrators of his major novels is thus almost infinitely complex and fluctuating.

On the other hand, it has become a commonplace of criticism that no novel is ever written in a vacuum. It is always written for the reader. Thackeray goes further: his novels are written not merely for, but to, even sometimes at, the reader. Surely the point need not be laboured. His fiction is a kind of conversation—however inevitably one-sided and spurious—with the reader and a game in which the reader becomes involved as the author's accomplice, whether he likes it or not. Thackeray himself described his work as 'a kind of confidential talk between reader and writer'.[1] Such an attitude was no novelty in English fiction, but it is probable that no one has proved as endlessly ingenious, evasive, disconcerting as Thackeray in his relationship with the reader.

An image of Thackeray's reader as seen by the writer can be built up by closely observing, on the one hand, his use of all sorts of personal pronouns (the *I* or *we* of narrator or author pitted against the reader's *you*; the *we*-sentences and the statements about *them* uniting author, reader and men in general); on the other hand, the novelist's allusiveness, either in the form of topicalities or in that of erudition. Thackeray is an educated man writing for educated people; he is a gentleman and a Londoner, writing for other gentlemen and city-dwellers.

What has been said so far applies by and large to Thackeray's fiction in general; most of it applies with particular force to *Pendennis*; almost none of it applies to *Esmond*.

[1] In his preface to *Pendennis*.

II

For clarity's sake, while considering *Pendennis*, it will be convenient to discuss Thackeray the craftsman apart from Thackeray the preacher.

The obvious source of the usual dissatisfaction with him as a craftsman is his unwillingness—some would say, his inability—to stick to his story. To give only one example at this stage, out of literally scores of possible illustrations, Chapter XVI has a long paragraph beginning: 'Thus, O friendly readers, we see how every man of the world has his own private griefs and business ...' It takes us twelve lines to be told that this refers to Mr. Smirke (who 'has a private care watching at his bedside'.) No sooner have we reached him than off we are again with '... and is no more satisfied than the rest of us. How lonely we are in the world! how selfish and secret, everybody! You and your wife have pressed the same pillow for forty years. ...' After the wife follow in quick succession 'your artless daughter', 'the honest frank boy', and even 'the old grandmother crooning in the corner ...' before we read, at the very end of the paragraph: 'Let us return, however, to the solitary Smirke.' It is not unfair, I suggest, to regard this as representative of Thackeray's peculiar narrative method, though it would certainly be unfair not to add that the paragraph as a whole is extremely interesting and contains general statements of an intellectual calibre above even Thackeray's average. Yet there remains the fact that, in some fifty lines, only the words 'Mr. Smirke has a private care' really belong to the narrative. All the rest is part of the conversation between author or narrator and reader, the reader being involved in his own person as well as through three or four generations of his relatives. Of course, if 'the story' is that of the relationship between reader and writer, no such objection can be made.

Uncertainty, or hesitancy, of another kind there is with regard to the narrator's omniscience. This conventional privilege is now exploited to the full, now flaunted, now disclaimed, often played with in a spirit of impish humour. There is less light-handedness in the frequent authorial comments accompanying Thackeray's overt manipulations of the narrator. He seems to be engaged in a constant, if half-hearted, attempt to justify the ways of the creative artist to the reading public.

Although there is a faint attempt, as we saw, to pretend that the narrator of *Pendennis* is distinct from the author, the relationship with the reader is partly established by Thackeray himself. An element of personal confession enters largely into all his fiction. *Pendennis* even contains the thinly veiled theory which justifies his practice in that respect: 'If the secret history of books could be written, and the author's private thoughts and meanings noted alongside of his story, how many insipid volumes would become interesting, and dull tales excite the reader!' (XLII). *Pendennis* is by no means a 'dull tale' or an 'insipid volume', but that may not be solely because the author did provide the kind of additional interest that a reader can derive from a sense of intimacy with the writer at work. Many of the first-person singular sentences are intrinsically uninteresting and non-committal when they come from the narrator, who is responsible, for example, for things like 'if, for my part, some kind friend tells me that such-and-such a man has been abusing me, I am almost sure, on my own side, that I have a misliking to such-and-such a man' (XX). But Thackeray occasionally forgets that he is using a narrator at all and his *I* becomes himself; writing Chapters LIII and LIV shortly after his own recovery from a serious illness, he turns his experience to good fictional account and even manages to thank his doctor and other friends through the medium of his novel.

The basic element of the novelist's attitude to both characters and readers is friendliness, which thus links or even fuses the two categories together. Not Pen alone, but at least fourteen characters, from Major Pendennis to Warrington, from Strong to Laura, are repeatedly referred to as 'my' or more frequently 'our' friend. The reader on his side is sometimes addressed as 'worthy friend' or referred to as 'the friendly reader'. The 'our' in 'our friend', whenever it is not a mere editorial possessive, involves the reader together with the author in an effusive mood. The author (or it may be the narrator) makes no mystery of his feelings towards the characters: he worships Helen, adores Laura, and is touched by Pen, whom he seems to be watching with anxious, quasi-avuncular care—possibly a not unusual attitude in real life to one's own younger self or selves. He addresses some of them, on occasion, as though he himself stood outside the story and was nudging the reader; but when he speaks of 'my young friend', he is resuming his place within the fictional world, and when he uses phrases like 'our catholic-minded young friend', he is asking us, his readers, to join him inside that world. At the very end of the book we are invited to give 'a hand of charity to Arthur Pendennis, with all his faults and shortcomings, who does not claim to be a hero, but only a man and a brother', and it is then clear that the hand of charity is to be extended, not to Pen alone, but to Thackeray and to ourselves as well. Pen is, so to speak, our 'mutual' brother.

Without being always quite so explicit, Thackeray uses other ways of channelling his readers' emotions. There is the method of the intrusive epithet, of which he is a great wielder. An intrusive epithet can be defined as an adjective intended to suggest a moral or sentimental judgment on any of the characters, over and above the conclusions which the reader may have formed from the said character's reported actions and speeches. Thackeray's intrusive epithets are roughly of two kinds: the ironical and the non-ironical. The non-ironical are the more truly intrusive— 'the insinuating, the wary, the wily, the selfish, Major'; or, about Laura, 'the honest and generous country girl'. The ironical epithets are less imperatively directive; Blanche is one of their main targets—'our little innocent Muse of a Blanche'; or 'this artless young creature'. The reader is left with the responsibility of interpreting such phrases. Two recurring epithets, 'worthy' and 'honest', sit astride the borderline between irony and non-irony.

There are enough fine passages in *Pendennis*, and the novel as a whole is sufficiently impressive, to make us feel that the author should not have been so unsure of himself or so hesitant as to his relationships with his characters and readers, whom he treats with a mixture, or rather an alternation, of affection and insolence. This makes it at times almost fatiguing to read *Pendennis*. The point of view is constantly shifting; the narrator's persona is elusive; and the reader is perpetually involved in—indeed, dragged into—the variety of games which it is Thackeray's pleasure to have him play. But it is hardly fair, he may feel, that he should be expected to play even a silent part in games of which the rules are not known to him; he may well suspect that the rules are not known to Thackeray either, that they are not complex so much as fluctuating, and that Thackeray permits himself to alter them at will, doing so without any clearer or more serious purpose than to amuse himself and us.

III

In one of the many paragraphs of moral commentary in *Pendennis*, Thackeray artlessly exclaims: 'Who has not preached, and who has practised?' (XLVI). In Chapter XXXVII of *The Newcomes*, he expounds a clear view of the novelist's proper province: 'the world, and things pertaining to it', not 'things beyond it', for 'Who is he that he should assume the divine's office, or turn his desk into a preacher's pulpit?' Yet when he paid one of his most charming tributes to Dickens, he described his own fiction as, in comparison, mere 'dismal preachings'[1]; and in a *Roundabout Paper* he confessed: 'Perhaps of all the novel-spinners now extant, the present speaker is the most addicted to preaching. Does he not stop perpetually in his story and begin to preach to you? ... I cry peccavi loudly and heartily.'[2] The fact is that Thackeray the novelist was an inveterate preacher, who loved preaching, even if it were (as it is in some of these examples) no more than preaching against preaching or against himself. It might be interesting to determine how far Thackeray's preaching in *Pendennis* harms the book and influences the author–narrator–reader relationship in that novel, by placing the novelist in a magisterial attitude to his audience.

In *Pendennis*, the narrator's stance is almost constantly that of a

---

[1] See 'Charity and Humour', *Miscellaneous Essays* (vol. XXV of *Works*, 1885, p. 371).

[2] Quoted by Arthur Quiller-Couch, *Charles Dickens and Other Victorians*, Cambridge, 1925, p. 139.

preacher or teacher. As a teacher he seems to be aware of the pedagogic value of iteration. Going one better on the principle laid down by the celebrated Snark-hunting captain who said 'What I tell you three times is true', he tells the reader at least four times that no one dies of frustrated love (in Chapters xv, xl, lvi and lxii). A similar number of comparable statements can be found in *Esmond*. Nor is the narrator of either novel much less sparing of his revelation that men are weak and erring creatures. Most of the innumerable digressions in *Pendennis* appear to result from the irresistible urge to impart to the reader information or advice, and the lessons of experience. The writer's moral instruction is usually aimed point-blank at the reader: 'Are these details insipid? Look back, good friend, at your own youth, and ask how was that?' we are told, typically, in Chapter iii.

Thackeray's moral teaching is roughly of two mutually contradictory kinds; there is on the one hand an indulgently cynical analysis of man in society, and on the other a regular course in theoretical morality. A clear example of the ensuing moral obscurity, or at least ambiguity, is provided by a cheap paragraph of the cheap episode (Pen at Vauxhall with Fanny, in Chapter xlvii, under the cheap heading 'Monseigneur s'amuse') where the narrator discusses kissing in general and defends himself against the possible charge of having hinted that Pen had kissed Fanny:

Not so. In the first place, it was dark . . .; secondly, he was not a man to have this kind of secret, and tell it; thirdly, and lastly, let the honest fellow who has kissed a pretty girl, say what would have been his own conduct in such a delicate juncture?

Well, the truth is, that however you may suspect him, and whatever you would have done under the circumstances, or Mr. Pen would have liked to do, he behaved honestly, and like a man.

The moral teaching here could hardly be more muddled and confusing. We are in effect told two things: (*a*) kissing girls is good sport and on the whole harmless enough; (*b*) there is a certain code of behaviour requiring that a man should refrain from kissing girls. We are invited to confess that under the circumstances *we* would doubtless have kissed Fanny; we are to be comforted by the admission that Pen would have liked to do the same; but we are also to be edified by finding that he did not do what he would have liked to do and eventually did instead what he thought he ought to do. The muddle lies in the assurance that Pen 'behaved honestly, and like a man' in not doing what 'the honest fellow who has kissed a pretty girl' had done so easily, naturally and, we may assume, pleasurably. Of course it would be rash to rule out the conjecture that the ambiguity is deliberate and the muddle wholly jocular. Yet the joke is at best laboured and the moral thinking uneasy.

There are at least 80 passages of moral generalization in *Pendennis*, where the generalizing procedures are diversified with considerable ingenuity. The purpose may be to comfort the reader labouring under the depressing sense of his own unworthiness by making him realize that he is no worse than other people. At the same time, however, the overall effect is of a destructive and dissolving kind: 'We and the rest of the world are poor creatures alike' (LXV); or, in the last sentence of the novel, we are invited to recognize 'how mean the best of us is'. This pessimistic view of mankind, this characteristically Thackerayan, *Ecclesiastes*-like mood will not be objected to because of its sombre nature, but the moral teaching may be resented because it is also hopelessly vague. The reader may be ready or even eager to be taught, but he will expect to be taught something definite. Now, when Pen's reluctance to marry Fanny is discussed (in Chapter LII), the pros and cons are adequately enumerated and balanced, yet at the end no firmer verdict is issued than 'in fine, let this be a reserved point, to be settled by the individual moralist who chooses to debate it'. Perhaps we ought to be grateful for the preservation of our liberty to decide after we have been duly enlightened. But this non-committal attitude is not easy to reconcile with the sense of moral responsibility expressed elsewhere—for instance, about the perilous effect on schoolboys and

students of having 'read and enjoyed Don Juan . . . Awful propagation of evil!—The idea of it should make the man tremble who
holds the pen, lest untruth, or impurity, or unjust anger, or unjust
praise escape it' (xx). Thackeray seems to be in earnest here; if so,
he may be held back, when he refrains from laying down moral
rules, by the fear of letting untruth or impurity escape from his
pen. He thus efficiently eschews the 'awful propagation of evil',
but he cannot be wholly acquitted of the hardly less awful
propagation of muddle-headedness and twaddle.

There remain, however, to embarrass the reader further, a
number of trashily grandiloquent passages about religious goodness and sanctity, usually in connection with Thackeray's notor-
ious, angel-like, good women. But he was by no means incapable
of rising to moral or philosophical reflections of real value, and
he does so many times in *Pendennis*, for instance on the difficulties
of communication among human beings (xvi) or of the quest for
selfhood (lx). But the various aspects of his moral thinking and
preaching are not reconciled and they fail to cohere into a con-
sistent and unified wisdom. At times, his various thoughts seem
to be addressed to different categories of readers, or to the same
reader at different times and in different moods (induced by
different episodes in the novel). Hence, perhaps, the bewildering
variety of names by which the reader is addressed in *Pendennis*.
Here is a brief selected list: 'yet tender mothers and sober fathers,
my good madam, worthy friend, O you spotless, O Clarissas of
this life, O thoughtless Dives, brother and sister'. The most
significant mode of address, we suggest, 'brother wearers of
motley', had already been coined in *Vanity Fair*. But in *Pendennis*
the relationship with the reader is thus made shifting and frag-
mentary.

The type of analysis and criticism applied to *Pendennis* in the
foregoing pages would not have been relished by the author, who
protests, in Chapter LIII, against 'those mischievous and prosaic
people who carp and calculate at every detail of the romancer'.
Having done very little so far except 'carp and calculate', the
critic stands rebuked: he has proved both mischievous and
prosaic.

IV

Thackeray's prophetic championship of his own cause has now received the perceptive and sympathetic support of what may be termed the Tillotson–McMaster plea for Thackeray's commentary, which has succeeded the traditional grumblings of earlier critics.

In 1954, Geoffrey Tillotson took up the cudgels against J. Y. T Greig in his *Thackeray the Novelist*.[1] His argument can be summarized briefly and illustrated by a few quotations here and there. He was out to 'Define the Thackerayan Oneness', which he found in 'The Materials' as well as in 'Form and Manner'. Tillotson made the admission that the oneness was virtual or potential rather than actual (p. 12). When he went on to inventory 'The Content of the Authorial "I"', Tillotson justified the use of the epithet 'authorial' by pointing out that in Thackeray's novels 'there is much of the "I" not belonging to any of his personages' (70). But it is in the chapter called 'The Author's Conduct of his Commentary' that Tillotson's most relevant assertions are to be found: 'The critic who likes Thackeray's novels must show that they are great without having their commentary shorn away; indeed he must show that they are greater because of their commentary. Unless he can maintain that, his praise of Thackeray might as well cease.'[2] So as to preserve the validity of his own praise, he then proceeds to assert, and indeed to a certain extent demonstrate, 'how universal in the passages of philosophy is narrative. Inside the passages of philosophy we are still seeing actions as well as receiving thoughts' (97). He shows that by exploring his own mind Thackeray enables his readers to know theirs better (231); yet, although the novelist is to be praised for 'an openness of mind, an untendentious readiness to see all sides

---

[1] Cambridge University Press. Greig's *Thackeray: A Reconsideration*, London, 1950, was frankly hostile to his author; many of his views were later rebutted by Gordon Ray and others. Greig's book was reprinted, however, as recently as 1967.

[2] The same point is made in somewhat more emphatic terms later: 'The critic of Thackeray . . . must stand or fall by the success of his proof that the novels would suffer from the loss of the commentary' (112), and 'if we read his novels at all, we must read every word of them' (113).

of a thing,' (236) 'with this intellectual fair-mindedness goes his
indecisiveness as a moralist. He lacks a burning need to rid himself
of vacillation, because matters seem to him, as to the ordinary man,
too mixed and obscure' (240). In the light of this other major
admission, it is tempting to object that 'the ordinary man' may
be as indecisive as he likes since he does not set up shop as a
professor of moral philosophy, whereas Thackeray does.

But it will be more interesting to take note of Tillotson's
constant use of the words 'author' and 'authorial', because it is at
this point that Dr. Juliet McMaster[1] usefully complements the
case for the defendant by introducing the vital distinction between author and narrator. Again, the outline of her argument
—or at least of that part of it which is relevant to this article, for
Dr McMaster brilliantly makes a number of other valuable
points—has to be described and illustrated by a few quotations.
Her contention is that Thackeray 'is a consummate artist very
much in control of what he is doing, whose major novels are
works of thematic coherence and aesthetic integrity' (vii). Like
Geoffrey Tillotson, she is an enthusiastic supporter of the
commentary: Thackeray's novels, she claims, 'live because of his
commentary, not in spite of it' (2). She sees in 'the unifying tone
of the narrator, a regular and reassuring reminder of the life and
harmony of the whole. For the life of the novel comes ... from
the tone and reactions of the man who tells the story; and more—
from the reader's own personal responses, elicited, though not
determined, by his' (2). She points out that Thackeray uses 'a
humanly fallible narrator' so that 'we have the sense that we are
being told the story by a fellow human being' (5). 'The passages
of commentary are not directives on what to think. Each is at
best only one way of looking at the matter; and the next may be a
different way, or emphatically the wrong one' (11).[2] Juliet
McMaster then lists and analyses 'the various roles that the author
chooses to play within the world of his characters' (12), and it

[1] *Thackeray: The Major Novels*, Manchester, 1971.
[2] At a later point Dr. McMaster again emphasizes her view that 'the voice
that seems to be telling us what to think ... is often a dramatic representation
of somebody else's reactions' (41).

seems to her that, by so varying his stance, he can 'involve us personally in the lives of his characters' (13), or again 'by inducing us to react, the commentary (which indeed *is* often inane, or smug, or gushing, as it is also often worldly and cynical) endows the characters with a kind of life, and makes us feel that they are autonomous beings with an existence beyond their creator's mind' (43). While later admitting that 'commentary, involving [a] rather dangerous process of breaking up the illusion of reality, is not good in itself' and that 'Thackeray himself, of course, was not always successful', she still thinks that his commentary 'at its best ... is not only entertaining and thematically relevant, but ... works as a sort of magic to build a bridge between us and the characters' (49). Some of Dr. McMaster's own readers may find it difficult to see how, by breaking up the illusion of reality, a sense of life can be achieved. Yet most of her suggestions are striking and call for a reconsideration of one's instinctive impatience.

Geoffrey Tillotson and Juliet McMaster, then, invite or compel a rereading and reappraisal of *Pendennis*. The large claims persuasively made by both do not however quite dispel all the reservations or dissolve all the contraditctions. One may still feel that a large part of the commentary comes from Thackeray himself, not from his chameleon-like narrator. When he says 'novelists are supposed to know everything', he is perhaps forgetting that his narrator is not supposed to be a writer of fiction; the only novelist in the case is Thackeray. The ghastly passage about 'awful propagation of evil' (xx) mentions 'the man ... who holds the pen' and his responsibilities, which are clearly, once more, the author's, not the narrator's. And when he explicitly—though not unambiguously—repudiates Warrington's views ('We are not pledging ourselves for the correctness of his opinions, which readers will please to consider are delivered dramatically, the writer being no more answerable for them than for the sentiments uttered by any other character of the story ...' (LXII), isn't he implicitly *not* repudiating the narrator's statements? It would be more pleasant to go all the way with Dr. McMaster's argument and believe that Thackeray dissociates himself from his narrator whenever the latter is turgid or foolish or nasty, but Thackeray himself does not allow us to do so.

V

Henry Esmond does not call for such pleading as *Pendennis* has demanded and obtained. *Esmond* is unquestionably a great novel, and one whose greatness has in fact seldom been questioned, except by some of its early reviewers. It is in many ways unlike Thackeray's other novels. In many ways, but not in all ways. Thackeray the craftsman and Thackeray the preacher remain true to type. There are artistic and technical flaws: cheap pastiches,[1] pedantry, inaccuracies, loose syntax, a regrettably half-hearted effort to use complementary or corrective footnotes; Rachel Castlewood bears some of the usual stigmata of Thackeray's saintly women, and thus does not always command the reader's full assent and sympathy, but then, unlike some of the others, she is clearly not intended to do so.[2]

As to the preaching in *Esmond*, though outwardly conducted by Henry, not by the author, it bears much resemblance to what we find in the other novels and is indeed sometimes couched in the very same words as elsewhere. Henry is on the whole more profound and serious than the narrator or narrators of *Pendennis*; yet when he writes 'From the loss of a tooth to that of a mistress there's no pang that is not bearable' (III-4), neither the idea nor the tone strikes us as a novelty. Henry's preaching, with the important exception of his views on time and memory,[3] is the usual mixed bag of mildly stimulating thoughts and worn truisms, of cynical and idealistic views, often toned down by uncertainty and self-questioning, of wisdom and worldly wisdom.

[1] I am not referring, of course, to the *Spectator* paper, but to the Dowager's broken French and Frank Castlewood's English spelling.

[2] One need not go to the explicit disparagement of Rachel in *The Virginians* to feel that, in *Esmond*, we are given, not an objective portrait but a reflection of the impression made on her enraptured and enslaved admirer, Henry; even so, the idealization is only intermittent.

[3] Admirably analysed by the late Henri A. Talon in 'Time and Memory in Thackeray's *Henry Esmond*', *R.E.S.*, New Series, XIII, 50 (1962). Shortly before he died, Professor Talon confided to me that he was writing—had in fact almost written—two other articles on *Esmond*.

There are however two major differences between *Henry Esmond* and Thackeray's other novels. One is that it was not published in monthly instalments: it was thus more carefully thought out as a whole before publication and considerably shorter than *Vanity Fair*, *Pendennis* or *The Newcomes*, for Thackeray was temperamentally incapable of resisting the temptations offered by periodical writing.[1] The other difference—more relevant to the theme of this article—is that the narrator tells his own story, though he tells it mainly in the third person. Admittedly, Henry is created and manipulated by Thackeray and is, in fact, much closer to the author than either Pendennis's 'historian' or Pen as Clive Newcome's biographer. In a way, by disguising himself as Henry, while making him very much like himself, Thackeray becomes freer than ever to express and confess himself. But from a technical point of view the advantage of the procedure is considerable: the narrator in *Esmond* is held with a much firmer hand than Thackeray's other spokesmen and can seldom wander about and play the endless games which more shadowy persons could indulge in. In other words, part of *Esmond*'s artistic superiority may consist in having a more stable, less impish narrator, whose relationship with author, other characters and reader is more definite than usual.

VI

In the preface to *Pendennis*, Thackeray wrote of himself: 'this person strives to tell the truth. If there is not that, there is nothing'. Well and good. Barring the apparent paradox of choosing fiction as a channel for telling the truth, few will quarrel with the unsensational principle thus expounded. But how far does the frequent *malaise* experienced by some of Thackeray's readers result from the novelist's inability to adhere to his own principle?

The feeling that his novels yield but fragments or facets of the truth is due in great part to a number of perfectly creditable motives. There are, for instance, deliberate subtleties and ambiguities; there are aspects of the truth which Thackeray knows he

[1] Even, unlike Dickens, the temptation of sprawling beyond the nineteenth or twentieth number.

cannot deal out wholesale but can merely encourage the reader to grope and struggle for. Hence the need not to be magisterial all the time. Nor should the critic complain of Thackeray's occasional, equally deliberate, refusal to choose, to commit himself, in complex matters, or of his usually indulgent attitude to the weaknesses of men and women, of which he had a clear perception, based mainly, it has been more than once suggested, on lucid self-knowledge. Again there can be nothing intrinsically wrong with such a sympathetic view, though it is disconcerting to find it coupled with moral exhortations.

Thackeray's constant use of irony is a further source of difficulty for the reader who knows that the writer aimed at telling the truth. Irony implies indirection and even, up to a point, duplicity. This complex alliance of contraries does not always work out well, at least in the interests of moral clarity and truth-telling.

But part of the *malaise* I have referred to also derives from characteristics that can only be entered on the debit side: there is a good deal of nonchalance in Thackeray the craftsman, of unsureness in Thackeray the moralist, so that the two main sides of his relationship with the reader are affected. The craftsman's nonchalance results in digressions, repetitions, loose ends and other signs of negligence. The moralist's unsureness produces contradictions and evasions.

In a striking passage of *Esmond* we read: 'there are a thousand thoughts lying within a man that he does not know till he takes up the pen to write' (II–I). It is true that taking up the pen to write is not infrequently a crystallizing process through which thoughts hitherto dormant become fully conscious, alive and articulate. Yet it is customary for a writer to think out his thoughts before he expresses them. Thackeray, however, believed it was his privilege to express—and his reader's to read—the 'thousand thoughts' that cropped up while he wrote, regardless of the fact that they could not be either a thousand different thoughts or a thousand germane ones: hence the tiresome iterations and the mutual contradictions—and the *malaise*.

Perceiving this is not tantamount to denying Thackeray's

enduring status as a great novelist. But it may help account for many readers' contradictory reactions, and also confirm the superiority of *Esmond*, a novel with a more immediate appeal than the others to the modern reader. This advantage was gained at the cost of some of the usual Thackerayan characteristics. The type of relationship he had achieved with his contemporary readers was so close as to make some sections of his work ephemeral: he addressed himself to them, not to us.

True 'Thackerayanness' will certainly go on being enjoyed by the class of readers who are sufficiently cultured not to object to Latin quotations and lavish displays of jocular French. Thackeray-addicts will also ever include the 'brother wearers of motley' invoked by the narrator of *Vanity Fair*. A brother wearer of motley is a man who does not mind being shown that he is a fool or a buffoon and thus enjoys the close relationship and identification with a writer without illusions, part mountebank, part highly intelligent analyst of the weaknesses of mankind, moving at a subdued moral level, using variegated lights, shapes and colours. Such a reader may well feel that, even where there is perplexity as well as complexity, he is eventually helped in his difficult effort to come to terms with his own foibles and with the human predicament.

Collective Intellect: Yeats, Synge and Nietzsche

LORNA REYNOLDS

My argument takes its start from the belief that there is no real quarrel between poetry and philosophy and that the great poet and the great philosopher of an epoch say essentially the same thing about man, the heart of man and human life. I suggest that we have a neat three-pronged illustration of this in the three great men whose names are included in my title.

The poets themselves have often claimed as much. So Coleridge in the *Biographia Literaria* wrote: 'no man can be a true poet without being at the same time a profound philosopher', Wordsworth in his famous Preface to the second edition of The *Lyrical Ballads* that poetry 'is truth [the traditional object of philosophical investigation] carried alive into the heart by passion', and Yeats, 'When I was a boy in Dublin I was one of a group who rented a room in a mean street to discuss philosophy. My fellow students got more and more interested in certain modern schools of mystical belief, and I never found anybody to share *my one unshakable belief.* I thought that whatever of philosophy has been made poetry is alone permanent, and that one should begin to arrange it in some regular order, rejecting nothing *as the make-believe* of the poets.'[1]

The philosophers, however, have been slow to acknowledge any kinship between themselves and the poets. But Nietzsche, 'the last thinker of the West' as Heidegger describes him, had no doubts about it:

Conscious thinking must be counted amongst the instinctive functions, and it is so even in the case of philosophical thinking;

[1] *Essays and Introductions* (London 1961), p. 65. My italics.

one has here to learn anew, as one learned anew about heredity
and 'innateness'. As little as the act of birth comes into consideration in the whole process and continuation of heredity,
just as little is 'being-conscious' *opposed* to the instinctive in any
decisive sense; the greater part of the conscious thinking of a
philosopher is secretly influenced by his instincts, and forced
into definite channels.[1]

Heidegger, who may in the future be regarded as the greatest
philosopher of our century, in his book *What is Called Thinking?*
states that academic philosophy has done its share to stunt the
meaning of the word 'thought', and taking his own point of
departure from the Old English word for 'to think', *thenkan*, and
its close relationship to *thancian*, 'to thank' (the word for thought
in Old English being *thanc*), he says: 'Compared with the root *thanc*,
thought in the sense of logical-rational representations turns out
to be a reduction and an impoverishment of the word that beggar
the imagination.'[2] Thought and thanks and memory, in
Heidegger's exposition, are all bound up with one another: 'Both
memory and thanks move and have their being in the *thanc*.
"Memory" initially did not at all mean the power to recall. . . .
Originally, "memory" means as much as devotion: a constant
concentrated abiding with something',[3] and it involves not only
the power of recall, but also the power of 'unrelinquishing and
unrelenting' retention:

> The 'thanc', being the memory so understood, is by the same
> token also what the word 'thanks' designates. In giving thanks,
> the heart gives thought to what it has and what it is. The heart,
> thus giving thought and thus being memory, gives itself in
> thought to that to which it is held. It thinks of itself as beholden,
> not in the sense of mere submission, but beholden because its

[1] *The Complete Works of Friedrich Nietzsche*, ed. Oscar Levy (Edinburgh and
London 1909), v (*Beyond Good and Evil*), 8. Subsequent references to this edition
will be specified under individual volume titles.
[2] Martin Heidegger, *What is Called Thinking?* trans. Fred D. Wieck and J.
Glenn Gray (New York 1968), p. 139.
[3] Ibid., p. 140.

devotion is held in listening. Original thanking is the thanks owed for being.[1]

Nietzsche and Heidegger, I suggest, write a gloss on Yeats's 'one unshakable belief', that 'whatever of philosophy has been made poetry is alone permanent'. Only when the *heart* thinks, giving thanks in thought to what it has and what it is, do we get poetry, and only then do we get philosophy. In short, poetry and philosophy are both manifestations of unity of being, of the total, thinking, feeling, remembering, thanking human being.

It is perhaps no accident that we had to wait until philosophers became interested in linguistics before they realized that no gulf separated the poets and themselves. For language has always been allowed to be the specific business of poets, language brought continuously by them back to the freshness of original meaning, through their really listening to what 'language says when it speaks', and what it undersays and oversays.

Everybody knows that at the turn of the century Yeats manifested a change in attitudes, in emphasis on different interests, and in style. He himself said many years afterwards, as 'I altered my syntax I altered my intellect'.[2] But syntax, being the arrangement of words in the sentence so as to bring out their relationship, if it is deliberate and not just traditional and un-thought out, must follow some idea of what one wants that relationship to be—must, in fact, come out of the intellect already altered. Syntax 'that is for ear alone',[3] 'a powerful and passionate syntax'[4], is how Yeats described the altered syntax. 'For the ear' implies the speaking voice, and 'powerful and passionate' implies intense and deeply moved speakers. Yeats's new syntax is the outward manifestation of the new attitudes, new emphases, new bearings of the man who had turned from absorption in the self to the drama of men in relation to one another and moved to a new stage of development.

[1] Ibid., p. 141.
[2] *Essays and Introductions*, p. 530.
[3] Ibid., p. 529.
[4] Ibid., pp. 521–32.

I want to suggest here that two other great men helped Yeats in this development. One was Nietzsche, and the other Synge, in whom I think he saw an embodiment of Nietzschean values.

It is customary to speak on these occasions of 'influence'. But I think that that implies far too passive a connection. It seems to me that we should rather speak of the delighted response of a spirit that thinks it is alone on a dangerous road and then suddenly sees someone who has travelled farther ahead and who stands beckoning him on. Yeats was quite conscious that he was changing with the new century, and specifically links this change with Nietzsche, thinking of it (obviously, when he had just read *The Birth of Tragedy*) as a change from the desire 'to get out of form' to the desire to 'create form'. 'Nietzsche,' he wrote to John Quinn, 'to whom you have been the first to introduce me, calls these the Dionysiac and the Apollonic, respectively. I think I have to some extent got weary of that wild god Dionysius, and I am hoping the Far-Darter will come in his place.'[1]

Nietzsche, looking up from the road he was on, had written in the Preface to the 1886 edition of *The Birth of Tragedy*: 'this book addressed itself to artists or, rather, to artists with analytical and retrospective leanings: to a special kind of artist who is far to seek and possibly not worth the seeking.'[2] In Yeats Nietzsche would have found an artist with analytic and retrospective leanings: in Nietzsche Yeats found the philosopher who was also an artist. Nietzsche, in one of his letters, talks of the need, if he is not to be lost, to make something precious of the bitter experience of rejected love as the need to turn 'muck to gold'. The constant activity of the artist is just this turning of muck to gold, either the actual muck of earth or the metaphorical muck of the soul, and Yeats, in fact, was confronted with just such a bitter experience, a lump of muck out of which he had to make gold. When he discovered Nietzsche, he found somebody who had trod ahead of him the same steps that he was himself on, who confirmed

[1] *The Letters of W. B. Yeats,* ed. Allan Wade (London 1954), p. 403.
[2] *The Birth of Tragedy and the Genealogy of Morals,* trans. Francis Golffing (New York 1956), p. 5.

what he apprehended, who carried him forward deeper in the channel into which he had been guided by Blake. He was delighted with his new guide and called Nietzsche a 'strong enchanter', and read him so avidly that his eye trouble worsened.

From then on it seems to me that the thinking of Nietzsche is entangled in most of Yeats's thinking. This is a vast subject and I can do no more than suggest certain lines along which it might be studied. There is a general diffusion and absorption of leading, indeed obsessive, themes and ideas; there are quite specific instances of the intellectual impression made by Nietzsche on Yeats. There is the continuation of the interest, as strong in 1930 as in 1904: there is an approval and adoption of emotional attitudes, and there is the help towards self-awareness by learning how the mind in creation works.

Let me give some samples of my first point. Such ideas as the essential unity of the human being, the falsity of the long-held dichotomy between body and soul, the passing of extremes one into another, the transcendence of established values, the need for the mask for self-understanding, the necessity to surpass oneself, satisfaction not as residing in the thing achieved but in the achieving, the concept of heroic joy, salvation from life's suffering through creation, the need for much suffering and much transformation before the creator can appear, the dance as the greatest expression 'of life's meaning', the admiration for the aristocratic virtues and contempt for the 'populace', the crookedness of the paths of wisdom, the inescapable duty of self-expression—all these are Nietzschean and they are also Yeatsian. If one read out of context the following passages to whom would one ascribe them?

Only in the dance do I know how to speak the parable of the higher things.[1]

Spirit is life which itself cutteth into life: by its own torture doth it increase its own knowledge.[2]

[1] *Thus Spake Zarathustra*, p. 133.
[2] Ibid., IV, 122.

That I have to be struggle, and becoming, and purpose, and cross-purpose—ah, he who divineth my will, divineth well also on what *crooked* paths it hath to tread![1]

Life is a well of delight; but where the rabble also drink, there all fountains are poisoned.[2]

By the study of those impulses that shape themselves into words without contest we find our thought, for we do not seek truth in argument or in books but clarification of what we already believe. It is for this reason that we hate those confident men and books who, as it were, trample in their top boots or crack their whips between our cradles. Dissatisfaction with the old idea of God cannot but overthrow our sense of order before the new conception of reality has even begun to develop, it is still a phantom not a child.[3]

No matter how full the expression, the more it is of the whole man, the more does it require other expressions for its completion.[4]

All truth is crooked; time itself is a circle.[5]

All energy that comes from the whole man is as irregular as the lightning, for the communicable and forcastable and discoverable is a part only, a hungry chicken under the breast of the pelican.[6]

The first four quotations and the seventh are from Nietzsche, the others from Yeats, but one might easily ascribe any one to either. Now let me point to some more specific instances, or resemblances. The poem *Lines Written to a Friend Whose Work Has come to Nothing*, with its exhortation to the difficult feat of turning pain to rejoicement, clearly celebrates a Nietzschean attitude:

[1] Ibid., IV, 137.
[2] Ibid., p. 113.
[3] W. B. Yeats, *Pages From a Diary Written in Nineteen Hundred and Thirty* (Cuala Press 1934), p. 24.
[4] Ibid., p. 17.
[5] *Thus Spake Zarathustra*, IV, 190.
[6] *Essays and Introductions*, p. 279.

Bred to a harder thing
Than Triumph, turn away
And like a laughing string
Whereon mad fingers play
Amid a place of stone,
Be secret and exult,
Because of all things known
That is most difficult.[1]

'Exult', that is, leap out of yourself, and do that when all around is stone, when no help comes from sensible objects. Do it, as if you were a string played on by mad fingers—that is, without reason. Do it in defeat, when your work has come to nothing—what is this but stoicism carried to ecstasy? And what is that but the 'short madness of happiness which only the greatest sufferer experienceth',[2] as Nietzsche's persona, Zarathustra, says?

At the end of *The King's Threshold*, the new man who is to replace existing man, Nietzsche's—I hesitate to use the word, for its meaning has been so distorted—superman, is celebrated:

O silver trumpets, be you lifted up
And cry to the great race that is to come.
Long-throated swans upon the waves of time,
Sing loudly, for beyond the wall of the world
That race may hear our music and awake.[3]

The underlying concept of *Where There is Nothing* is thoroughly Nietzschean—the concept of the necessity of destruction as a prelude to recreation. And what are the following lines, from *A Prayer for my Daughter*,

Considering that, all hatred driven hence,
The soul recovers radical innocence
And learns at last that it is self-delighting,

[1] *Collected Poems*, p. 122.
[2] *Thus Spake Zarathustra*, IV, 32.
[3] *Collected Plays*, p. 143.

Self-appeasing, self-affrighting,
And that its own sweet will is Heaven's will,[1]

if they are not an embodiment of the Nietzschean belief that
hatred, or revenge, which is the natural consequence of hatred, is
part of the human will's enslavement to time and dependence
upon that from which it really wishes to make itself independent;
and that once freed from hatred, the human being can realize
itself as rooted in itself and fulfil itself in unity with primal being?
To quote Heidegger, glossing Nietzsche:

> Deliverance from revenge is the transition from the will's
> revulsion against time and its 'It was', to the will that eternally
> wills the recurrence of the same and in this willing wills itself as
> its own ground. Deliverance from revenge is the transition to
> the primal being of all beings.[2]

It is easy enough to see the relationship in such instances. But
what is one to make of the terrifying parable in Part III of *Thus
Spake Zarathustra*, called 'The Vision and the Enigma', and its
possible connection with *The Second Coming*? In 'The Vision and
the Enigma' Zarathustra, ascending his strong mountain with the
Dwarf, the spirit of Gravity, on his shoulders, has his vision of
two roads, one running backwards to eternity and the other for-
wards to eternity, and a realization that they must meet, and
hence of necessity bring back the same moment in an eternal
cycle of recurrence of all things. Immediately after this he hears a
dog howl blood-curdlingly. He goes to see what is making the
dog howl and finds a young shepherd with a serpent half-in and
half-out of his mouth, and cries to the young man to bite its head
off. I quote:

> Solve for me the enigma that I then beheld, interpret unto
> me the vision of the lonesomest one!
> For it was a vision and a foresight:—*what* did I then behold
> in parable? And *who* is it that must come some day?

[1] *Collected Poems*, p. 214.
[2] *What is Called Thinking?*, pp. 104–5.

Who is the shepherd into whose throat the serpent thus crawled?

Who is the man into whose throat all the heaviest and blackest will thus crawl?

—The shepherd however bit as my cry had admonished him: he bit with a strong bite! Far away did he spit the head of the serpent—: and sprang up.—

No longer shepherd, no longer man—a transfigured being, a light-surrounded being that *laughed*! never on earth laughed a man as *he* laughed!

O my brethren, I heard a laughter which was no human laughter,—and now gnaweth a thirst at me, a longing that is never allayed.[1]

If we now listen to *The Second Coming* we realize that it might have been called *The Vision and the Enigma*:

> Surely some revelation is at hand;
> Surely the Second Coming is at hand.
> The Second Coming! Hardly are those words out
> When a vast image out of *Spiritus Mundi*
> Troubles my sight: somewhere in sands of the desert
> A shape with lion body and the head of a man,
> A gaze blank and pitiless as the sun,
> Is moving its slow thighs, while all about it
> Reel shadows of the indignant desert birds.
> The darkness drops again; but now I know
> That twenty centuries of stony sleep
> Were vexed to nightmare by a rocking cradle,
> And what rough beast, its hour come round at last,
> Slouches towards Bethlehem to be born?[2]

Yeats's vision is of a creature, half-man, half-beast, Nietzsche's of a transfigured man, but transfigured by the horrible experience of biting in two the serpent stuck in his throat, a laughing, light-surrounded figure. Nietzsche's creature transcends man; Yeats's is a brute supplanter. But is there not something similar in both presentations, one called a vision, the other a revelation, which

[1] *Thus Spake Zarathustra*, IV, 193.
[2] *Collected Poems*, p. 211.

means an unveiling, so that what is there to be seen may be seen, in the dropping of the darkness after the moment of revelation in Yeats and the rousing of the never-allayed longing caused by the vision in Nietzsche? Both writers question their vision. *Who* is the shepherd, *who* is the man, *what* rough beast? The enigma remains unanswered in both. As with this poem, so with many others, their deeper resonances may be perceived by knowing Nietzsche.

I turn now to the remarkable resemblance between the way Nietzsche and Yeats dramatize their processes of mind. Neither thinks in abstractions. Both believe that conflict is essential to thought, as to all other manifestations of life. Yeats in *The Diary of Nineteen Thirty* puts it this way:

> I am trying to understand why certain metaphysicians whom I have spent years trying to master repel me, why those invisible beings I have learned to trust would turn me from all that is not conflict, that is not sword in hand. Is it not like this? I cannot discover truth by logic unless that logic serve passion, and only then if the logic be ready to cut its own throat, tear out its own eyes—the cry of Hafiz. 'I made a bargain with that hair before the beginning of time?' the cry of every lover. Those spiritual beings seem always as if they would turn me from every abstraction. I must not talk to myself about 'the truth' nor call myself 'teacher', nor another 'pupil'—these things are abstract—but see myself set in a drama where I struggle to exalt and overcome concrete realities perceived not with mind only but as with the roots of my hair. The passionless reasoners are pariah dogs and devour the dead symbols. The clarified spirits *own* the truth; they *have* intellect; but we receive as agents never as owners, in reward for victory.[1]

A drama in which reality is mastered and exalted, that is, made great by nourishment, lifted up, refined, through being perceived by the whole man, even to the roots of his hair—that is the process of thought as seen by Yeats. Nietzsche saw it the same way and once said it in a wonderfully succinct aphorism: 'Write with

[1] *Pages from a Diary*, p. 15.

blood and you will find that blood is spirit.' For both of them this realization of the processes of thought as dramatic and as involving the whole man meant inventing symbolic figures who are, as it were, the acting out of their thought. In *Thus Spake Zarathustra* a crowd of such figures come on the scene. A mere listing of them—the two wise kings, the magician, the soothsayer, the serpent, the eagle, the hunchback, the dwarf, the beggar, the shadow, the old woman, the ugliest man—is sufficient to show how close they are to the symbolic figures of Yeats's interior drama, his inner world.

Part of this drama, which man is forever acting out within himself, is for both Nietzsche and Yeats the giving of style to his character, the treating of himself as if he were a work of art. 'To "give style" to one's character—a great and rare art!' Nietzsche wrote in *The Gay Science*:

> He practises it who surveys all that his nature presents in strength and weakness and then moulds it to an artistic plan until everything appears as art and reason, and even the weaknesses delight the eye. Here a large amount of second nature has been added, there is a piece of original nature removed. . . . It will be the strong, imperious natures which experience their subtlest joy in exercising such a control, in such constraint and perfecting themselves under their own law.[1]

We must become what we are by finding the laws of our own nature and consciously striving towards its perfection: we must exercise our own power against ourselves and so find the limits of our endurance: we must push ourselves beyond ourselves, in the self-awareness and self-possession which is part of man's way of being. 'It is always inexcusable,' Yeats said, 'to lose one's self-possession' and 'In daily life one becomes rude the moment one grudges to the clown his perpetual triumph.'[2] In fact, Nietzsche and Yeats saw life and thought as a continuous experiment of

[1] Quoted in R. J. Hollingdale, *Nietzsche, The Man and his Philosophy* (London 1965), p. 173.
[2] *Autobiographies* (London 1961), p. 463.

recognition—'das Leben ein experiment des Erkennenden sein durfe'—[1] and of creation. 'I want to teach men the sense of their existence,'[2] Nietzsche has Zarathustra say. The artist is the man who best understands this and best exhibits it in his own life.

About the same time as Yeats was reading Nietzsche and finding him a 'strong enchanter' he was also getting to know the man whom he was to call 'that rare, that distinguished, that most noble thing, which of all things still of the world is nearest to being sufficient to itself, the pure artist'.[3] We have to understand these words in the light of the Nietzschean man who, by facing and understanding reality, mastering and exalting it, transvalues values. In the essay from which I have just quoted Yeats tells us that Synge was the only Irish writer who, since perhaps Maria Edgeworth in *Castle Rackrent*, had written in a way to change a man's thought about the world, or stir his moral nature. For the others, he wrote,

> but play with pictures, persons and events, that whether ill or well observed are but an amusement for the mind where it escapes from meditation, a child's show, that makes the fables of his art as significant by contrast as some procession painted on an Egyptian wall; for in these fables, an intelligence on which the tragedy of the world has been thrust in so few years that Life had no time to brew her sleepy drug, has spoken of the moods that are the expression of its wisdom. All minds that have a wisdom come of tragic reality seem morbid to those that are accustomed to writers who have not faced reality at all.[4]

This is clearly the highest praise. Synge is chosen as the first modern Irish writer who instead of painting the surface of life, an activity possible merely by exercising the faculty of observation, chooses out of his concentrated experience of the tragedy of the world, by means of his art, fables in which a deep-lying wisdom is unfolded. In short, Yeats suggests that the facing of tragic reality is wisdom; the expression of it is art; and that Synge is the first

[1] *Die fröhliche Wissenschaft*, Buch ii, p. 321.
[2] *Thus Spake Zarathustra*, IV, 16.
[3] *Essays and Introductions*, p. 323.
[4] Ibid., p. 322.

modern Irish tragic artist. I believe that Yeats was absolutely right in so describing Synge. The Greene and Stephens biography shows how he spent so much of his short life searching for a medium of expression, thinking first it would be music and only late coming to the realization that it would be language; how he also sought, through isolation and study and wanderings at home and abroad for this understanding of reality which Yeats praises. Everybody knows how Yeats sent him to the Aran Islands, but not everybody realizes how he had prepared himself for what he was to perceive there. There is a great deal to be said on this subject, but this is not the place. Here I should like to point out that Yeats, like everybody else, is wrong when he talks about Synge as a writer of peasant plays. Synge did not use peasants as characters. What Synge did was to write about a primitive community, that is, a community living in accordance with habits of thought and behaviour once characteristic of all the human race. His characters are the people found in such communities; fishermen, nomads (tramps and tinkers), holy men, lonely women, hunters, kings, queens, and warriors. What he also did was realize that such people's habit of thought is animistic; and Synge's famous language is a way of giving expression to such habits of thought. It, like himself, is pure art: it is 'artificial,' in the proper sense of the word, not the result of accidental observation but of deliberate invention, not to be found spoken in any part of Ireland, though animistic habits of thought linger on in country parts, though vivid imagery still marks Irish country speech and the simplest Irish people love learned words, in however distorted a form they may reach them. In short, the language of Synge's people is an 'ideal' or universal Irish one, not a real dialect.

Such a people and such a language enabled Synge to keep clear of all clichés and all stereotypes and write with supreme originality and at the same time deal with the 'fundamental realities of life'. He was quite clear that that was the business of drama. 'No drama', he wrote to Stephen McKenna, 'can grow out of anything but the fundamental realities of life which are never fantastic, are neither modern nor unmodern and, as I see them, rarely spring-dayish, or breezy or Cuchulanoid. . . .' He goes on:

I think squeamishness is a disease, and that Ireland will gain if Irish writers deal manfully, directly and decently with the entire reality of life. I think the law-maker and the law-breaker are both needful in society—as the lively and volcanic forces are needed to make earth's crust habitable—and I think the law-maker is tending to reduce Ireland, or parts of Ireland, to a dismal morbid hypocrisy that is not blessed unripeness.[1]

Poetry, drama, Synge is saying, as Aristotle did, deals not with what has happened but with what may happen, because of the nature of fundamental realities. Fundamental realities are fundamentally tragic, and involve destruction, but to face this is to be the opposite of morbid: not to face it is hypocrisy, or a kind of drug-taking, as Yeats suggests.

But to face it requires extraordinary strength of spirit, as Nietzsche pointed out:

It is the business of the very few to be independent; it is the privilege of the strong. And whoever attempts it, even with the best right, without being *obliged* to do so, proves that he is probably not only strong, but daring beyond measure. He enters into a labyrinth, he multiplies a thousand fold the dangers which life in itself already brings with it; not the least of which is that no one can see how and where he loses his way, becomes isolated and is torn piecemeal by some minotaur of conscience.[2]

It is immensely to Yeats's credit that he recognized Synge as such a free and strong spirit. 'In one thing he and Lady Gregory are the strongest souls I have ever known,' he wrote:

He and she alike have never for an instant spoken to me the thoughts of their inferiors as their own thoughts. I have never known them lose the self-possession of their intellects. . . . Both Synge and Lady Gregory isolate themselves, Synge in-

[1] David H. Greene and Edward M. Stephens, *J. M. Synge 1871–1909* (New York 1961), p. 163.
[2] *Beyond Good and Evil*, v, 43.

stinctively . . . so instinctively and naturally . . . that no one is conscious of rejection.[1]

Yeats wrote this when Synge was in his last illness, and Yeats wondered if perhaps Synge's 'purity of genius', his inability to think anybody's thought but his own, to write of Ireland out of anything but his own loving perception, his quarrel with the 'wreckage of Young Ireland', might not bring him to his death. And he compares himself with Synge and feels that if he too had kept himself free of 'the influence of Young Ireland', he might have given a 'more profound picture of Ireland' in his work.[2]

Synge's life, it would seem, illustrates for Yeats the Nietzschean concept of the artist's conscience which has become a commonplace of modern thought:

The tension of soul in misfortune which communicates to it its energy, its shuddering in view of rack and ruin, its inventiveness and bravery in undergoing, enduring, interpreting, and exploiting misfortune, and whatever depth, mystery, disguise, spirit, artifice, or greatness has been bestowed upon the soul—has it not been bestowed through suffering, through the discipline of great suffering? In man *creature* and *creator* are united: in man there is not only matter, shred, excess, clay, mire, folly, chaos; but there is also the creator, the sculptor, the hardness of the hammer, the divinity of the spectator, and the seventh day.[3]

Whether Yeats had read these words of Nietzsche in 1909 I do not know, but he certainly saw Synge as such a creature and creator. He tells us explicitly that Synge affected his whole way of work, that he had thought to do for Ireland what the Young Ireland poets had done, only in a more profound way, until Synge began to write. Then he saw 'that we must renounce the deliberate creation of a kind of Holy City in the imagination and

[1] *Autobiographies*, p. 473.
[2] Ibid., p. 472.
[3] *Beyond Good and Evil*, v, 171.

express the individual',[1] that his business was not to build ideals for the people of Ireland, but to look at the people of Ireland and express their life—that was the way to find the real, which is also the only true ideal; and Synge showed him the way.

Most of the great men of an age share something of the same qualities of intellect. What I have been suggesting is that the philosopher Nietzsche expressed certain ideas about the nature of life, the processes of thought, the conscience of the artist, which the poet Yeats welcomed as his own, seeing in them an elaboration of Blake's ideas; and that Synge became for Yeats a living embodiment of the conscience of the artist, as expounded by Nietzsche. It is immensely to Yeats's honour that he recognized this and learnt from Synge. All three writers came to an understanding of the essentially dramatic nature of human life, of the interior life of the individual as much as of the external encounter of individual and individual. If we wished to describe this in a sentence we could hardly do better than use Yeats's words: 'Man can embody truth but he cannot know it.' All three are modern writers in the sense that their thought is with us still and that we are still struggling with the necessity to see life as constant change and ourselves as constantly having to remake ourselves, each one needing the morality of the artist in his attempt to 'turn muck to gold'.

[1] *Autobiographies*, pp. 493–4.

VII

Old Writers and Young Readers

GEOFFREY TREASE

'FORTY years on' is a good moment for personal stocktaking. It was in 1933 that, burning my boats (not for the first time), I forsook the dubious security of a teaching post and turned my twenty-fourth birthday into a triple anniversary by getting married and becoming a full-time free-lance writer. That so much of the writing was fated to be for children was something I never foresaw and would have dismissed as almost too improbable to be worth considering.

I was not interested in children. I had just been teaching for a year, admittedly, but those two statements imply no inconsistency. In the depressed nineteen-thirties what embryo writer did not earn his bread, and deepen his depression, by serving for a spell in some kind of private, often comic, boarding school? Day Lewis, Auden—most of them did it. It was part of the apprenticeship.

Nor did children's literature present itself, even to the most desperate struggler, as a promising field in which to win fame and fortune. Of fame there was none for the living. Children's books were in the doldrums. With a handful of exceptions such as A. A. Milne, no writer enjoyed any public esteem. 'You can't beat Henty and Ballantyne,' was the cry. Every one looked backwards. There was such a dearth of criticism that if, once in a while, a new children's author of originality appeared, his advent was scarcely noticed. *Swallows and Amazons* came out in 1930 and *Mary Poppins* in 1934, but it was years before the names of Arthur Ransome and P. L. Travers meant anything to me.

If there was no fame, there was not much fortune. Children's books were commonly published under the old system long

abandoned for other types of book. The author sold his copyright
for a single payment of perhaps fifty pounds. There was nothing
to be done then but begin another, and then another. He was on
a treadmill. It was small wonder that so much of children's
literature was hackwork.

Two motives, none the less, impelled me to enter this
unpromising field. One was that great spur to inspiration,
financial need. Even fifty pounds was a fortune when an article
earned only a couple of guineas. The second motive was political.

It was not only the spell of schoolmastering that I shared with
Day Lewis, Auden and so many others, it was the Left-wing
idealism of that generation, which in my own case had drawn me
to a short-lived membership not of the Communist but of the
Independent Labour Party. Now, living far from London and its
political excitements, I found another outlet for my feelings. I
was already aware, from my not-so-distant boyhood, that boys'
fiction was, as George Orwell was to declare seven years later,
'sodden in the worst illusions of 1910', and I would certainly have
agreed with him when he continued, 'The fact is only unimportant
if one believes that what is read in childhood leaves no impression
behind.' With this in mind, I wrote to a publisher with a con-
spicuously Left-wing list and inquired if he would be interested in
adventure-stories with a Socialist slant.

What about Robin Hood, I asked? It was an obvious suggestion, especially from a native of Nottingham like myself. Children
should realize, I argued, that Sherwood would have been a grim
place in January, and that there had been unromantic compulsions
to adopt the outlaw life. Some of the merriment should be taken
out of Merrie England. The story would gain, not lose. You
could stand Henty on his head without taking the kick out of
him. Indeed, the inverted position was often a stimulus to vigorous
activity.

Such was the genesis of *Bows Against the Barons*, published early
in 1934. Though a first book of fiction, by an unknown beginner,
it was accepted somewhat unusually on a synopsis and three
chapters. Before I knew where I was, the label of 'children's
author' was riveted upon me. Yet there was a practical incentive

for continuing along the path upon which I had stumbled. My publishers' Marxist principles forbade the exploitation even of authors and there was an unquestioned acceptance of the royalty system, at least in the context of the book trade. So, although sales were small and it was years before the royalties reached the sum I should have received for an outright sale of my story, I was led on by the hope of jam tomorrow.

How did one write for children? To entertain them was essential. At that date I knew there was a prejudice against historical fiction, which was associated with compulsory holiday reading, long-winded descriptive passages, and archaic diction, especially in the dialogue. There were too many varlets crying 'quotha!' Too many writers slipped into a stilted, didactic style which set up an unnecessary barrier between them and their readers. A conscientious author of those days, Gertrude Hollis, in *Spurs and Bride*, would produce a sentence like this:

'Yonder sight is enough to make a man eschew lance and sword for ever, and take to hot-cockles and cherry pit,' exclaimed the Earl of Pembroke, adding an oath which the sacred character of the building did not in the least restrain.

An obliging footnote informed the young reader that 'hot-cockles and cherry pit' were 'popular games'.

The avid young book-lover might accept this kind of thing on the terms stated by one child, Gillian Hansard, who expressed herself thus honestly: 'Though the details of Scott's novels are not always correct they give one a very good idea of the period, and though they are rather painful to read they always give benefit.' For most children, however, this was too suggestive of a visit to the dentist. There was a widespread resistance to historical fiction, and somehow it had to be broken down.

One thing was clear. Ye olde jargon must go. In my own schooldays I had discovered Naomi Mitchison's splendid early novels, *The Conquered* and *Cloud Cuckoo Land*. I had realized what living dialogue could do. I had felt the truth of Ernest Barker's approving comment on her method, 'These ancient figures must break into modern speech if they are to touch us.' I did not know that, as I set my Sherwood outlaws talking like ordinary human beings, Robert Graves was simultaneously doing the same with his Romans in *I Claudius*, which also came out in 1934. Yet for all the influence of that famous novel and its sequel, ye olde jargon lingered for a long time. One could still find characters crying 'I joy me' and even 'Wot you what?' while a writer of such future distinction as Carola Oman might be caught lapsing into an unguarded *mélange* of archaic and contemporary: 'I am not in a great hurry, if you truly desire aught, but I think I ought to be turning home now.'

Apart from a resolution to keep away from Wardour Street, I had no confident formula for winning over a juvenile public. I would simply write for them, I told myself, as I would write fiction for adults, but leaving out the sex. The passage of forty years has modified both the general principle and the exception.

Granted, it is fatal to write down. 'When you write for children,' said Anatole France, 'do not adopt a style for the occasion. Think your best and write your best.' That is a splendid thought, something to cling to in hesitant moments, but for the practising craftsman it is not a sufficient guide.

Granted, too, that the 1973 ten-year-old is more sophisticated than his counterpart forty years ago, and in some respects genuinely more mature, which is by no means the same thing. Childhood, to many people's regret, has been telescoped into a much shorter period by varied factors ranging from earlier puberty to the pressures of television and advertising.

Grant that in any generation children may be more intelligent than their parents, more literate, better informed (especially about new scientific and technical developments), and more fully endowed with that quality of 'apprehension' which Walter de la Mare distinguished from 'comprehension'.

Grant all this, yet the writer is left with one obvious and inescapable difference between child and adult readers: the former have not lived so long, and in the nature of things they cannot have built up the same mental and emotional capital of background knowledge and first-hand experience. They were not alive fifteen years ago. To them, 'all our yesterdays' are already history that has to be learnt.

Thus, in writing an introductory biography of D. H. Lawrence for those school-children who now quite early encounter some of his work in class, I recently had to remind myself continually that the Nottingham of his youth, and of my childhood, was almost as remote to them as Periclean Athens. The clanking, swaying electric trams, the open market stalls with their scents and colours, the pleasure steamers at Trent Bridge, the steam trains puffing into the city from all those vanished local stations—the whole background of *Sons and Lovers* and *The White Peacock*, which it is unnecessary to establish for the adult reader, has to be touched in, discreetly, for the adolescent. 'Discreetly', because he must be neither bored nor affronted by too overt explanations. But if the author is to communicate effectively he cannot risk making too many assumptions. Can he rely, for instance, on all his young readers—especially in the United States—knowing that when Lawrence went to school Queen Victoria was still on the throne, a fact not irrelevant to his story? Can they place George V—or the Kaiser? The author who writes without some such awareness of his readers' age-group is asking for trouble.

This is not to say that every 'i' must be dotted. A book, Alan Garner has said, 'must be written for all levels of experience.' There must be, as he rightly insists, a text that works 'at simple plot level', to make the reader turn the page. 'Anything else that comes through in the book is pure bonus. An onion can be peeled down through its layers, but it is always, at every layer, an onion, whole in itself. I try to write onions.'

The onion metaphor is admirable. In forty years the frontiers of children's literature have been pushed back far beyond any horizon I could see in 1933. The comic old taboos have gone. I can recall the time when 'books for boys' and 'books for girls' were as carefully segregated as lavatories, when 'healthy reading' involved unlimited carnage but not the least hint of tenderness between the sexes, and when a Nonconformist editor rapped my knuckles for permitting two adults and four adolescents to consume a single bottle of Sauternes with their Christmas dinner. 'Is it right,' he demanded, 'to introduce children to the cocktail habit?' That was in 1952.

Now almost nothing is barred in a children's book, and it may reasonably be asked whether the pendulum has not swung too far, for the very reason already stated, that the child reader has *not* lived very long and is inevitably handicapped by a lack of first-hand experience which only time can supply. When I read in a *New Statesman* review, of a 1971 story for older children, that 'the crisis scene is first intercourse, the boy making a mess of it, and thinking himself impotent', I shudder to think of the effect upon some boys reading the book. Another recent book dealt with 'a series of promiscuous affairs . . . backstreet abortion . . . adolescent homosexuality'. The tale of a mother's suicide, told from the standpoint of her eleven-year-old son, was recommended in a specialist journal concerned with children's books as 'most suitable perhaps for the nine to eleven-year-olds'.

I prefer the onion. The individual child peels off just as many layers as his stage of maturity impels him to.

Even in their externals, the life of D. H. Lawrence and the life of Byron (which I wrote for young readers previously) offer good stories, rich in incident, character and colourful background. Even the outer layers of the onion have savour and some nutriment. Yet it would be impossible to write the biographies in question and evade such central topics as Augusta Leigh and 'Lady Chatterley'. Their significance goes into the inner layers of the onion. A child mature enough to have grasped the meaning of, say, homosexuality or incest does not need to find the actual words, much less their definitions, when he reaches Byron's time at Cambridge or his association with his sister. He will read fluently between the lines—as he will, similarly, when he reads of Lawrence's tortured love affairs with Jessie Chambers and Louie Burrows, or *The Rainbow*, or the police raid on Lawrence's phallic paintings. The less mature reader will have no information thrust upon him that he is not ready to absorb. Biography for children is an excellent medium for learning about life, in some ways perhaps even better than fiction, but its author must not be expected to include a manual of sex education at the same time. As most sex educationists themselves view with disfavour the premature answering of questions the child has not asked, the 'literary onion' seems the right form in which an imaginative writer should present his work to the young.

It is also the most personally satisfactory. One need feel no restrictions. The book can be as good and as deep as the author's mind. As has often been remarked, no first-class children's book has ever failed to hold countless adult admirers. Given the story-telling craft to get the outer skins right—exciting, mysterious, fantastic, or what you will—the author is free to put his own heart and soul into the rest.

It would be misleading to convey the impression that sex was the only, or principal, subject on which we can now write for children with a freedom unknown when I began. As long ago as 1946 a New Zealand librarian, Dorothy Neal White, could say, in her study *About Books for Children*: 'Children's literature has changed inwardly. It has broadened its range and increased its depth . . . slowly maturing, as modern knowledge—political science, sociology, anthropology, economics—all impinged upon it.' Today, after a generation of further change, amounting to nothing less than a revolution in this field, no theme that attracts the sufficiently gifted writer can be ruled out summarily as unacceptable. To recall Anatole France again, 'Think your best and write your best' is a safe principle.

When I chose to begin with a Robin Hood story I was deliberately taking a hackneyed theme not from commercial caution but for the fun of turning it upside down. Later I did the same thing with the Cavaliers, and with the aristocrats in the French Revolution. But there is another pleasure, no smaller, in choosing a subject unknown to most children and opening a window to show them a world completely fresh—Moorish Spain, Norway in the time of the Hanseatic League, Urbino under the good Duke Federigo, even the old Birmingham Bull Ring in 1839, with Chartists and redcoats locked in battle.

Various factors determine the selection. Some historical events seem of such transcendental importance that, if they are being ignored by other children's writers or (one feels) wrongly presented, it appears almost a duty to relate them. Such, for me, was the Bolshevik Revolution, which I treated in a story called *The White Nights of St Petersburg*, though in a rather different manner from the one I would have adopted thirty years earlier. The desire to make political propaganda faded long ago. It is right that a children's author should have something to say in his books, and desirable (in my view) that he should speak on the side of freedom and justice. Partisan preaching is another matter. One of the differences between writing for adults and writing for children is the special responsibility which the latter involves. The adult reader is assumed to be fit to look after himself, able in theory at least to challenge the author's controversial views and verify his statements from other sources. The writer for adults is entitled, if he pleases, to argue a case like a barrister. The writer for children, however, has the same moral responsibility as a teacher. Even though his young readers demand heroes and villains he must still try—in presenting historical issues—to give the devil his due.

So, nowadays, the great political struggles of the past are only some of the themes that inspire me, and even they tend to be combined with some other, quite different, kind of inspiration. I fall under the spell of a character, like Garibaldi, and write *Follow My Black Plume* and *A Thousand for Sicily*. Or a period and setting, Mantua and Urbino in the *quattrocento*, and the result is *Horsemen on the Hills*. Even the Bolshevik story, when at last I got to writing it, drew much of its life from the loveliness of the setting in which those messy events took place—it was the first-hand memory of white nights beside the Neva in 1935 that provided the necessary spark of poetic inspiration to keep the typewriter clicking in 1966. And in writing *Trumpets in the West*, while I wanted to tell young people about the Glorious Revolution I was no less eager to tell them about the period when the English were a truly musical nation. I can still remember my delight, as a plot-maker, when I discovered a handy coincidence of dates—William of Orange's arrival in London occurred within a month or two of the first English opera, Purcell's *Dido and Aeneas*. Since the latter was presented at a girls' school in Chelsea, nothing could have slotted more neatly into a children's novel.

Often the second theme, which can contribute so much of the depth and vitality of a story, springs not from the period but from today. I can quote two very obvious examples from my own experience. The 'historian's motive' for writing *Mist Over Athelney* was the desire to tell children that our Anglo-Saxon fore-fathers had not been as 'rude' as old-fashioned teaching used to depict them and that pre-Conquest England enjoyed in many respects a civilization finer than what immediately succeeded it. Alfred, the book-loving fighter, was the obvious hero, Alfred, the wearer of that splendid jewel we can still see in the Ashmolean. The eventful months before and after Athelney offered the obvious frame for the plot. But the second theme, the driving force to write the story, came from the television newsreel, showing night after night the queues of prospective emigrants outside Australia House and similar offices. It was 1957. We were going through one of our wearisomely recurrent economic crises. The popular cry was 'England is finished!' It was parroted by those interviewed in front of the camera, one heard it everywhere. I heard it myself alarmingly, from young people all too near and dear. I knew that the same cry had been heard in Wessex in 878. Guthrum seemed master of the last Christian corner of England. Alfred was 'missing, presumed dead'. In Dorset and Hampshire the dispirited English were loading their portable possessions into ships and getting out, across the Channel, while the going was good. They had been mistaken. The twentieth-century English could be mistaken too. *Deor's Lament* provided an apt text: 'That passed. This also may.'

My other example is the highly topical theme of racial and religious toleration. I had long wanted to use an Andalusian setting and to depict for children the period when Arab culture had transformed southern Spain into a garden, later spoilt by the neglect of its Christian conquerors. The then-tolerant attitude of the Arabs to the Jews, in striking contrast to the persecution practised by the Catholics, added a further dimension. Requiring a link with England, to make the theme less remote to my young public, I dated the story in 1289 and 1290, when Edward I expelled the Jews from his realm. Convenient coincidence once more took a hand: during those months the King and Queen Eleanor—whose final illness was also most convenient, because I wanted to work in Jewish medicine and Arab pharmacy—spent much of their time in Nottingham Castle. Thus, for the opening chapters, I could return to the familiar ground of Sherwood Forest and medieval Nottingham where my very first book had been set.

That was not so labour-saving as it sounds. The medieval town which Robin Hood entered in *Bows Against the Barons* was little more than a painted backdrop. The Nottingham depicted thirty-two years later in *The Red Towers of Granada* was a patient reconstruction, as faithful as I could make it. I knew where the tiny ghetto stood, the Carmelite convent, the river wharf where the Franciscans unloaded their barges, Lister Gate where the dyers lived, Bridlesmith Gate, Fletcher Gate, every cobbled lane and the trade that was plied there.

Historical accuracy was never more important in the children's story than it is now. Any flaw will be detected, and gleefully, by some one. I spent great pains on my Anglo-Saxon story. It passed publishers' readers and reviewers unchallenged. Then came a letter from a small boy in Aberdeen. I had described the flight of my young characters from Guthrum's winter quarters in Gloucester and, with an Ordnance Survey map of Roman Britain beside me, I had traced every yard of their journey along the snow-covered Fosse Way, *but*—in a moment of aberration—I had allowed them to sup on rabbit, stewed over a camp-fire; and, as the young Aberdonian severely reminded me, rabbits had reached England only with the Normans.

Research must be thorough, but it must also be thoroughly absorbed by the author. It must be integrated in character and action, it must not show obviously in explanatory passages which the reader will instinctively skip. Research is one of the joys of writing for children, but it also has its perils, for too much is as bad as too little. The writer must beware of falling in love with charming period details that tickle his own adult taste. He must resist the temptation to 'work them in' when they do not further the action and will only slow it down.

Sometimes the research required for some adult volume provides both the idea and the ready-made background material, so that there is very little additional 'homework' to be done. The Garibaldi stories were born of my general history of Italy, *The Italian Story*, and after writing *The Condottieri* for adults it was truly child's play to transmute the same material into the fiction of *Horsemen on the Hills*. In the process of research for a history of my native city I found fresh ideas crowding into my mind for stories, set in various centuries, that would bring the workaday life of an English provincial town alive for young readers. It was, indeed, the work needed for *Nottingham, A Biography*—research in greater depth than I had been previously accustomed to—that opened my eyes to fresh possibilities and set me wondering, a shade guiltily, whether I had not neglected the history of my own country and been too often attracted by exotic settings elsewhere. Children, however, need both to discover the treasure under their feet and to gaze on far horizons, so their authors may fairly do the same.

In any case, the writer must begin by pleasing himself and choose his theme accordingly. The communication of his own interests and enthusiasms is his function. Today he is fortunate in that, unless those interests and enthusiasms are very odd indeed, he has unprecedented freedom to communicate them to the young.

Freedom of subject-matter is matched with freedom of style. There are still people, no doubt, who imagine a children's writer as one cruelly limited in vocabulary. Such people cannot have opened any recently published children's books. They might have found, had they done so, an exuberance of language too seldom present today in the matter-of-fact pages of the adult novel with its drab, tape-recorded dialogue. As one critic has said of Leon Garfield, 'He treats the English language with a mastery that sometimes verges on outrage . . . Leon Garfield can do anything with words and his touch is very sure.' It is true that, shortly after the Second World War, some publishers were frightened by certain educationists into acceptance of the theory of 'vocabulary limitation' or 'word control', which had begun like so many theories in the United States but was already losing ground there. It did not make much headway in Britain. Academic surveys of children's comics and playground speech soon confirmed what teachers and parents had always known, that children had a surprisingly, sometimes alarmingly, extensive vocabulary at their disposal. The storyteller need not ration himself, but that is not to say that, in addressing the young, he would not be well-advised to bear in mind some special considerations. But I have always felt that these were a stimulus to better writing rather than a handicap.

As a schoolboy on the Classics side, I was taught to admire the Greek and Roman preference for concrete rather than abstract expression. Children share this preference. One writes no worse for studying their taste. The dead metaphors that litter our casual language are a double evil when they appear in prose for children, for, while the adult reader can step over the corpses without noticing them, some children are always meeting a particular dead metaphor for the first time and will not recognise it as such. The previous sentence is a good example of how not to write for children.

Elliptical expressions and obscure (however witty) allusions will most often be blemishes in prose intended for understanding by the young, and for the same reason. They are intelligent enough and the subtler television plays have quickened their recognition of 'flash-backs' and other imaginative tricks, but, just as they have not lived long enough to acquire much historical background, so even the brightest cannot yet have acquired the linguistic equipment to catch every nuance of meaning that an older person can be relied upon to pick up. But English is none the worse for being simple, direct and unambiguous. Nor is there any need to rule out, in their proper place, those colourful, evocative, incantatory passages which supply the element of the 'rich and strange', as vital to enjoyment as complete and literal comprehension. Garfield, afore-mentioned, and a host of other talented writers are the proof of that.

Writing for children involves two other special considerations, which in turn carry with them their particular challenges and rewards. A good children's story must stand being read aloud and it must bear repetition. How many adult novelists need worry about, or hope for, either test? Yet what an encouragement they are to get one's prose just right.

A story may be read aloud by any one from a radio professional to a stumbling school-child in class. It should generally be possible to achieve a style that will create no difficulties for the child yet at the same time offer scope for the actor to display his skill. In revising his manuscript the author becomes alert to detect those awkwardnesses, embarrassments sometimes, which the silent and solitary reader would scarcely notice.

An absurd little example will illustrate this. Writing of Garibaldi's defence of Rome in 1849, I wanted to emphasize Mazzini's personal humility, which I felt would help to endear him to children. Bolton King's biography described how, when installed in the magnificence of the Quirinal Palace, the revolutionary leader 'hunted for a room small enough to feel at home in'. In my original draft I was careless enough to translate this into dialogue and make his young admirer exclaim, 'He is the most important man here and he is using the smallest room in the palace as his office!' Ancient memories of the classroom saved me. As I re-read those words I heard, in imagination, the roar of laughter that would have gone up from any group of children to whom they were read aloud. Similarly, though I could not avoid naming the palace once, there was such a risk of the accent being placed on the wrong syllable that I was not having any more 'Quirinals' than necessary.

The second incentive to careful writing has only to be stated: whereas few adults read the same novel twice, it is common for a child to read a favourite story half a dozen times, often with a lapse of years between, which gives extra force to the onion-layer analogy. Whole phrases and sentences are remembered at that impressionable age. As many a subsequent autobiography has revealed, they remain part of the reader's mental furniture for life. They ought to be good.

Perhaps we think too much about the classroom aspects of children's literature. The writer cannot afford to forget them, because the school library and the special school edition provide so much of his livelihood. Forty years ago, most teachers believed that the only good author was, like an Injun, a dead one. All that is marvellously changed. The living author is read and invited to lecture to courses. He is made the subject of flattering 'projects' and receives, with mixed feelings, batches of children's letters demanding answers to questions which with proper guidance could have been found in the reference library.

There is a danger, however, that the role of the children's author should be regarded as educational, not artistic. Clearly, there is an overlap. So there is with Shakespeare, but Shakespeare is more than an educational tool. So, in his humbler fashion, is the children's author. He may write better than many a novelist—or he may *be* a novelist, in which case he does not stop being a literary artist when he turns to address a younger audience. Yet our histories of English Literature commonly ignore children's books as if they did not exist. In Legouis and Cazamian, for example, there is space to mention the obscure Elizabethan Thomas Hughes but no word of the man who gave us *Tom Brown's Schooldays*.

The past forty years have seen a miraculous flowering of children's books and a welcome improvement in the status of their writers, but there is still a tendency to patronize them as second-class citizens in the commonwealth of letters. They deserve better. There is nothing easy about writing for the young. Boswell admitted that long ago, when he made one of his many unfulfilled resolutions, in this case to write some day 'a little story-book' like the ones he had enjoyed as a boy.

'It will not be an easy task for me,' he noted, 'it will require much nature and simplicity and a great acquaintance with the humours and traditions of the English common people. I shall be happy to succeed, for he who pleases children will be remembered with pleasure by men.'

Like 'The Other', 'Good Night' and 'The Unknown Bird', these poems illuminate and confirm the fearlessness of his self-scrutiny (equally apparent in his intimate, personal poems) and his refusal to accept false comforts from apparently 'blissful' moments spent in the contemplation of natural scenes. Blessed with a heightened visual response to the seen world, he was no captive to his powers of perception: his time scale remained simultaneously momentary and geological:

> No offence. Doubtless the house was not to blame,
> But the eye watching from those windows saw,
> Many a day, day after day, mist—mist
> Like chaos surging back—and felt itself
> Alone in all the world, marooned alone.
>
> There were whole days and nights when the wind and I
> Between us shared the world, and the wind ruled
> And I obeyed it and forgot the mist.
> My past and the past of the world were in the wind.
> Now you may say that though you understand
> And feel for me, and so on, you yourself
> Would find it different. You are all like that
> If once you stand here free from wind and mist.

This was that 'cloud-castle' which he constantly pitted against what others would call 'real' events: 'But flint and clay and child-birth were too real, For this cloud-castle.'

In some such internal debate as this the *persona* of his effective poems was developed, providing the necessary external observation-post from which he could check fancy against fact, contemplation against abstraction and, above all, his deep puritanical obsession with duty against his natural instinctive response to an emotively apprehended consciousness of 'beauty'. The new peace that his friends attributed to his enlistment was surely born from the new power that he experienced, through his poetry, to come to terms with those moments of significance in his past life which had previously eluded adequate expression:

> Once the name I gave to hours
> Like this was melancholy, when
> It was not happiness and powers
> Coming like exiles home again,
> And weaknesses quitting their bowers,
> Smiled and enjoyed, far off from men,
> Moments of everlastingness.
> And fortunate my search was then
> While what I sought, nevertheless,
> That I was seeking, I did not guess.

Sensitive to natural phenomena like sleep and dark and the rhythm of the seasons and, equally responsive to long-scale changes sustained by forests and heaths, he seems to have selected the wind as one of his personal symbols for joy in the powers of self-expression, a power external to his own brooding nature:

> My heart that had been still as the dead tree
> Awakened by the West wind was made free.

There is no better epitaph to his life than this and no clearer guide to his poetic development.